IMAGINE HOUSTON

VOLUME IV

PRODUCED BY PUBLISHING RESOURCES, LLC

SEAMLESS INTEGRATION | The glorious Houston Skyline District emphasizes the multifaceted cityscape that is the hallmark of ongoing redevelopment in downtown Houston. The natural beauty of green spaces is incorporated into the 21st century skyscraper architecture for a perfect blend of modern authenticity.

Downtown Loft Living

The Sabine Street Lofts Apartments on the rejuvenated Buffalo Bayou area in downtown Houston are a prime example of the high quality of life offered by living in the nation's fourth largest city. The bayou rejuvenation included a new $15 million waterfront park with hiking and biking trails, 12 street-to-bayou access points, native landscaping, civic artwork and picnic lawns.

Imagine Houston

VOLUME IV

Introduction	8
Quality of Life	10
Downtown	10
Surrounding Downtown	34
Uptown	52
The Woodlands	60
Clear Lake	68
Galveston	72
Major Events	78
Museums & the Arts	110
Dining	132
Shopping	138
Sports	142
Education	150
Texas Medical Center	160
Infrastructure	172
Energy	178
Profiles of Success	185

Publishers, Carlo van der Burg and Gilles van der Burg • Account Executive, Stephanie Olmstead and Ashlee Kahn
Editorial, Victoria Hyla • Art Director, Michael Weber • Artwork and Layout, Alejandra Varghese
Advertising Production Coordinator, Rebekah Wratchford • Photography, Charles Edwards
Distribution and Accounts Receivable, Cecile Ruffino

© 2011 Publishing Resources, LCC

Imagine Houston (ISBN 978-0-9816394-2-0) is published by Publishing Resources, LLC, 1415 Louisiana, Suite 3475, Houston, TX 77002. Copyright © 2011 by Publishing Resources, LLC. The information in this publication is gathered in such a way to ensure maximum accuracy. Publishing Resources, LLC cannot and does not guarantee the accuracy of all information furnished, or the complete absence of errors and omissions; hence no responsibility for the same can be, or is, assumed. All rights reserved. No part of this publication may be reproduced or reprinted without the written consent of Publishing Resources, LLC. The editor is not responsible for unsolicited contributions.

INDUSTRY PILLARS | Houston is synonymous with the energy industry and its companies that do business in the city. Many well-known organizations have a strong presence in the downtown skyline like the magnificently gleaming Chevron Towers, which are recognized for their fluid shape and luminescence.

Restored Glory

Showcasing Houston's unique place in the world

Welcome to the fourth edition of **Imagine Houston**! This 2012 edition is another tribute to our thriving, energetic city and the many beautiful vistas that those of us living here know so well but that might surprise longtime residents, newcomers and visitors alike.

Nowhere is Houston's entrepreneurial and can-do spirit better captured than in its diverse business community. Featured in the latter pages of the book, you will find a "Who's Who" of Houston's most successful companies and business professionals that have written our city's success story the way it is. We hope that their stories are an inspiration to you and that Houston, as presented in this edition, instills an even greater sense of pride in everyone that turns its pages.

Publishing Resources offers its creative services to the various media outlets owned by our family as well as hundreds of companies and media outlets across our nation. Our longtime staff photographer, Charles Edwards, once again has captured the majority of the photographs in these pages. They showcase the splendid combination of imagery that our buildings, parks and people provide that make up the multifaceted fabric of our beloved Bayou City. For the first time, Victoria Hyla has written the captions and many of the Profiles of Success that you will read, and we also would like to thank Cecile Ruffino, Michael Weber, Alejandra Varghese, Rebekah Wratchford, Stephanie Olmstead and Ashlee Kahn for their contributions and efforts working with the companies spotlighted in the book. Without all of them, **Imagine Houston** would not be possible.

If you are new to Houston or visit it often, **Imagine Houston** has been presented to you as a gift. We trust that you will enjoy the vivid depiction of this vibrant city as much as we do. If you are a Houstonian receiving this book, we hope we are able to surprise you with a few new ways to look at our timeless city and inspire you to contribute to a bigger and better Houston.

Enjoy.

Gilles van der Burg
Publisher

Carlo van der Burg
Publisher

Restored Glory | Recently renovated to its old glory, the Julia Ideson Building, named after one of the city's most dedicated librarians is a classic example of the influence of Spanish Renaissance architecture in Houston nestled among towering modern giants. Home to the Houston Metropolitan Research Center, the building received listing in the National Register of Historic Place in 1977.

Plentiful Parks

Houston has many parks located in the shadows of downtown, such as the tree-filled Buffalo Bayou Park. Other natural areas in the urban landscape include Memorial Park, Market Square Park, Discovery Green, Hermann Park and Tranquility Park, which are just a few of the popular recreational spaces utilized daily by thousands of Houstonians.

DOWNTOWN FUN

Houston Pavilions has introduced world-class shopping and dining venues into the downtown area, making after-work gatherings fun and convenient. During the week, Houstonians take advantage of special events happening downtown, including seasonal treats like an ice skating rink or outdoor summer movies.

Discovery Green

Downtown Houston's redevelopment has created some of the most interesting recreational venues in the city, including Discovery Green, a 12-acre park featuring a lake, interactive water features, an amphitheater stage and two dining facilities: The Grove and The Lake House.

CITY LIVING — With Houston's improved city transportation, redeveloped downtown parks and family-friendly gathering points, living in the heart of the city offers many advantages for those looking to live in high-rises and lofts.

ECLECTIC ENTERTAINMENT — In addition to traditional events that Houston hosts regularly, unconventional projects like the Houston Illuminated Art Car Parade, also known as Gloworama, give residents something new to enjoy. With the use of 3D mapping by LD Systems, striking visuals are projected on the George R. Brown Convention Center while dazzlingly lighted cars parade by.

DOWNTOWN DIVERSITY | Downtown Houston's diverse roster of venues has made it a top destination for events. Among them are Houston's House of Blues location with its private member club, The Foundation Room, and Houston-native Beyoncé's personal favorite, the House of Deréon Media Center. Houston boasts many other indoor event spaces, such as the nightclub Venue Houston, as well as stunning outdoor spaces like the rooftop pool at Four Seasons Houston.

DOWNTOWN REVAMPED — Houston's downtown area offers something for everyone. The Houston Pavilions feature world-class shopping and dining venues. The popularity of organic produce has resulted in an increased presence of outdoor markets like the one at Discovery Green. The new recently revamped Sabine to Bagby Waterfront Park now attracts year-round events in the shadow of Houston's dominant skyline.

LIVING LARGE — Pedestrian-friendly walkways and conveniently located apartment complexes in downtown and the vicinity allow for a growing urban population. Luxury high-rise buildings, such as the sophisticated and architecturally distinctive One Park Place, are continuing to push the boundaries of urban living, making it a truly remarkable experience.

CIVIC BEAUTY | The reflection pool in Hermann Square in front of City Hall provides the perfect assembly place for the Urban Harvest Farmers Market as well as festivals, corporate gatherings and other celebrations.

ARCHITECTURAL AESTHETICS | Nestled amid the surrounding Houston skyline, Tranquility Park is an example of the city's charm. Parks like this pop up in unexpected but welcome locations, as do trees and other flower plots, which beautify the city streets and contribute to keeping the city green and clean.

Bayou City Synergy

With more than 5,000 energy-related firms, Houston often is referred to as the Energy Capital of the World. Global companies, such as Shell, Chevron, Hess Corporation and Exxon Mobil Corporation, have a major presence downtown, creating the third largest skyline in the United States.

Perfected Parks — Downtown Houston's Market Square Park received a $3 million facelift in 2010 with the addition of a dog park and the Niko Niko's restaurant, making the park great for family gatherings. Other downtown parks feature trails that allow for more strenuous activities, such as running, biking and hiking along Allen Parkway and the bayou.

PULSATING METROPOLIS — The iconic downtown skyline provides a picturesque backdrop for Houstonians as they travel around the city. No matter what time of day or night, with so many wonderful things to see and do, the city always is buzzing with activity.

ATHLETIC PURSUITS

With an increased awareness about health and wellness, Houstonians are proving that they can be just as fit and active as their counterparts on the West Coast. The city features a number of excellent areas for kayaking, biking, hiking, jogging and running as well as outdoor sporting venues.

Western Edge

Just west of downtown along the Buffalo Bayou Park and Allen Parkway, a variety of developments, including high-rises, apartment buildings and condos, give urbanites wanting to see the city skyline but not live in it a perfect combination of nature and city. Scattered throughout are various parks and paths great for outdoor activities.

Crowning Achievement

Located three miles from downtown Houston, the 32-story Royalton at River Oaks provides commanding views of the city's skyline while architecturally distinguishing itself with its iconic crown.

DISTINCTIVE DISTRICTS The new West Ave mixed-use property and nearby retail and dining options converge at two of Houston's most celebrated districts: River Oaks and Upper Kirby. River Oaks, the area between downtown Houston and the Uptown District, is an exciting, reinvigorated environment making way for outdoor eateries and boutique shopping.

LUXURIOUS LIVING The Art Deco–inspired West Ave development captures the spirit of the surrounding neighborhood while offering a contemporary collection of cafés, fine-dining establishments, boutiques, luxury apartment homes and more. Regional and national brands create the ultimate one-stop-shop for fashion, dining, mingling and pampering in the heart of the Bayou City.

CULTURAL TRANQUILITY

Just south of downtown within walking distance of the Texas Medical Center is Hermann Park. The historic 445-acre public green space is home to many enjoyable experiences, such as the peaceful Japanese Garden, the family-friendly Miller Outdoor Theatre and the eight-acre McGovern Lake where visitors can rent pedal boats.

CAN-DO SPIRIT — Across from the Houston Museum of Natural Science sits a monument to Sam Houston, the city's founder and namesake. Embodying the can-do spirit of Houstonians, the statue anchors Hermann Park, which offers visitors a natural respite in the Japanese Garden or on a scenic tour of the park on the Hermann Park Railroad.

RELIGIOUS DIVERSITY

Houston is home to many iconic places of worship with faiths as diverse as their architectural styles. Some have been around for nearly a century, like St. Paul's United Methodist Church, which was completed in 1930 with a bell tower reminiscent of the Stone Gothic style of many European cathedrals. Others are more recent, such as the Catholic Co-Cathedral of the Sacred Heart, dedicated in 2008. Its modern exterior is Indiana limestone, Calcutta Gold marble and Fatima Beige limestone.

Uptown Business Uptown is home to more than 2,000 companies and 2 million square feet of office space, making it the 17th largest business district in the United States. Uptown is anchored by the Williams Tower, Texas' fourth tallest building and Houston's tallest outside of downtown. It was built in 1983 as a monumental symbol of the era of Houston energy companies showcasing their success.

UPTOWN LIVING | Residents of the Uptown area have the choice of a plethora of upscale living facilities with diverse architectural styles in the immediate vicinity of the Galleria mall. Also highly visible is the large concentration of residential high-rises built during a mini boom in the late 1990s.

EQUESTRIAN DELIGHTS | Founded in 1928, the Houston Polo Club is dedicated to the sport of polo and equestrian activities. Situated on 26 beautifully landscaped and wooded acres, the club is part of the social fabric of Uptown and is open to anyone wanting to enjoy its recreational and social amenities.

Uptown Flow — One of Houston's most lavish areas and a center for high-end retail and dining, Uptown also features a stunning architectural piece, the Williams Waterwall. Designed by award-winning architect Philip Johnson, the semicircular fountain is one of the city's most beloved landmarks, rising 64 feet and sending approximately 11,000 gallons of water over both sides of the wall every minute.

Town Center | Considered the "downtown" of The Woodlands community, Town Center brings an urban feel to the otherwise residential focus of The Woodlands with its paved streets, shops, restaurants, hotels, office buildings, lofts, town homes and condominiums.

CONTINUED GROWTH | Dedicated in 1974, The Woodlands is located 28 miles north of Houston and has a population of 100,000. It continues to grow as a community, not just for residents but also for many corporations. Among its most recognizable features is the Woodlands Waterway, which is based on the famous San Antonio River Walk.

SERENE SANCTUARY

The Woodlands continues to garner attention as a premier master-planned community with an exceptionally high standard of living and pleasing aesthetics. Job opportunities and the addition of several corporations' headquarters have made the Houston suburb ideal for savvy professionals.

FAMILY FESTIVITIES

The quality of life in The Woodlands is visible in its many events and activities in Town Center and other public areas. Events range from seasonal festivals like the Woodlands Waterway Arts Festival; the Red, Hot & Blue Festival; and the Lighting of the Doves Festival to casual family outings in the lushly designed public spaces.

WATER BOUND — The Clear Lake area is defined by the bodies of water in and around it. With an affluent population nearing 150,000, the area is both a thriving business community and home to one of the largest concentrations of recreational boats and marinas in the nation.

WATERSIDE RETREAT — Nearby Seabrook, Texas, offers a tranquil respite from the rigors of metropolitan life. Sailing is a frequent pastime for local residents, and the city attracts a significant number of visitors due to its location and recreational amenities.

GALVESTON MARVELS

Galveston is a popular getaway for Houstonians and tourists because of its beautiful beach setting, lush and luxurious hotels and historically rich landscape, which includes the Hutchings Sealy Building built in 1895. The famed Moody Gardens complex provides education and entertainment at its aquarium, rainforest and science pyramids and its IMAX 3D Theater.

RICH HISTORY — Since the devastation of Hurricane Ike in 2008, Galveston and The Strand Historic District have returned to a state of prosperity with tourists visiting and enjoying annual festivals like the famous Mardi Gras parade. Listed by the American Institute of Architects as one of the 100 most significant buildings in the United States, Bishop's Palace is a crowing jewel of the city's East End Historical District.

SEASIDE PORTAL — The Port of Galveston regularly fills the 36 blocks of its social and shopping center, the historic downtown district called The Strand, with cruise passengers starting or finishing their coastal adventures. Along the popular Seawall Boulevard, the 1900 Storm Memorial remembers the victims lost at sea during the great hurricane of that year.

Revolutionary Pride

The San Jacinto Monument embodies the historical relevance on which Houston was founded. Located in nearby LaPorte on the San Jacinto Battleground, the monument commemorates the site and this defining moment of the Texas Revolution.

COWBOY CULTURE — Every spring, the Houston Livestock Show & Rodeo celebrates traditional Texas heritage with the largest event of its kind in the world, opening with a 10K Rodeo Run and Downtown Rodeo Parade. Heralded by floats and marching bands, trail riders from all corners of Texas assemble at Memorial Park to celebrate with a party of their own before converging on downtown.

HOUSTON TRADITION — Reliant Stadium is home to the Houston Livestock Show & Rodeo's popular concert series. Reliant Park also serves as the site of the carnival fairgrounds, which features rides, games and hundreds of booths showcasing an assortment of daring foods as well as down-home Texas cooking.

COMPETITIVE NATURE | Beyond the rodeo competition, a goal of the Houston Livestock Show & Rodeo is to provide scholarships to deserving students. Open competitions invite students from the farm country to showcase their livestock, which are judged by set criteria to determine the finest specimens. Winners receive scholarships to the university or institution of higher education of their choice.

URBAN COWBOYS | The Houston Livestock Show & Rodeo has evolved into an impressive annual event that draws headliners from all genres to perform at Reliant Stadium. When musical acts are not on stage, 21st century cowboys are competing for the $1.5 million in cash prizes.

UNITED TOGETHER — The city's annual Fourth of July festival, Freedom Over Texas, invites all Houstonians to partake in a celebration of liberty and community. Live concerts, food and entertainment mark this star-spangled extravaganza. The full day of festivities is punctuated by one of the largest and most impressive fireworks displays in the country.

GIVING THANKS | Established in 1949, the Houston Thanksgiving Day Parade now has 3,000 participants preparing a show for nearly 400,000 spectators. The parade's main attractions are a procession of floats, giant balloon figures, marching bands and drill teams that fill the streets of downtown Houston with Texas pride.

Running Together The heart of downtown marks the starting point for various running races in Houston. Opening the Houston Livestock Show & Rodeo is the 10K Rodeo Run. At the Chevron Houston Marathon, an annual event in which more than 20,000 people run, participants can become fundraisers for one of the more than 50 listed charities as they embark on this extreme yet rewarding physical challenge.

Bayou Races — Water enthusiasts utilize Houston's rejuvenated Buffalo Bayou year round. Two events dominate the calendar: the Buffalo Bayou Regatta, Texas' largest canoe and kayak race, and the Houston Dragon Boat Festival, which promotes awareness of the Asian and Asian-American culture.

Celebrating Diversity

Cultural diversity is one of Houston's notable attributes, with dozens of festivals, such as the Houston International Festival, commemorating cultural groups from all over the world. Multipurpose venues also make it possible for the city to host high-profile sporting events in a variety of disciplines.

Art Car Parade

A Houston tradition since 1988, the Houston Art Car Parade is the first and largest in the world. All along Allen Parkway, the parade showcases a spectacle of many types of vehicles decorated in various colorful themes as well as classic cars, low riders and other highly modified vehicles.

FLYING HIGH — Held at the NASA/Johnson Space Center, the annual Ballunar Liftoff Festival is a celebration of the human fascination with and quest for flight. In addition to more than 80 giant hot air balloons, the festival features skydivers, hang gliders and aerial acrobatics of all kinds.

Flying Aces

The nation's fifth largest air show, Wings Over Houston, has taken place at Ellington Airport for the past 27 years. Each year, visitors can get up-close views of mammoth air machines as well as see shows, including vintage-plane reenactments like the Pearl Harbor attack and demonstrations of the U.S. Air Force's newest fighter jets.

FASHION FORWARD | Meeting and event planners converge on Houston to host and attend high-profile events and savvy affairs, such as Houston Fashion Week. Multifunctional indoor and outdoor spaces bring new life to events not normally held in innovative venues.

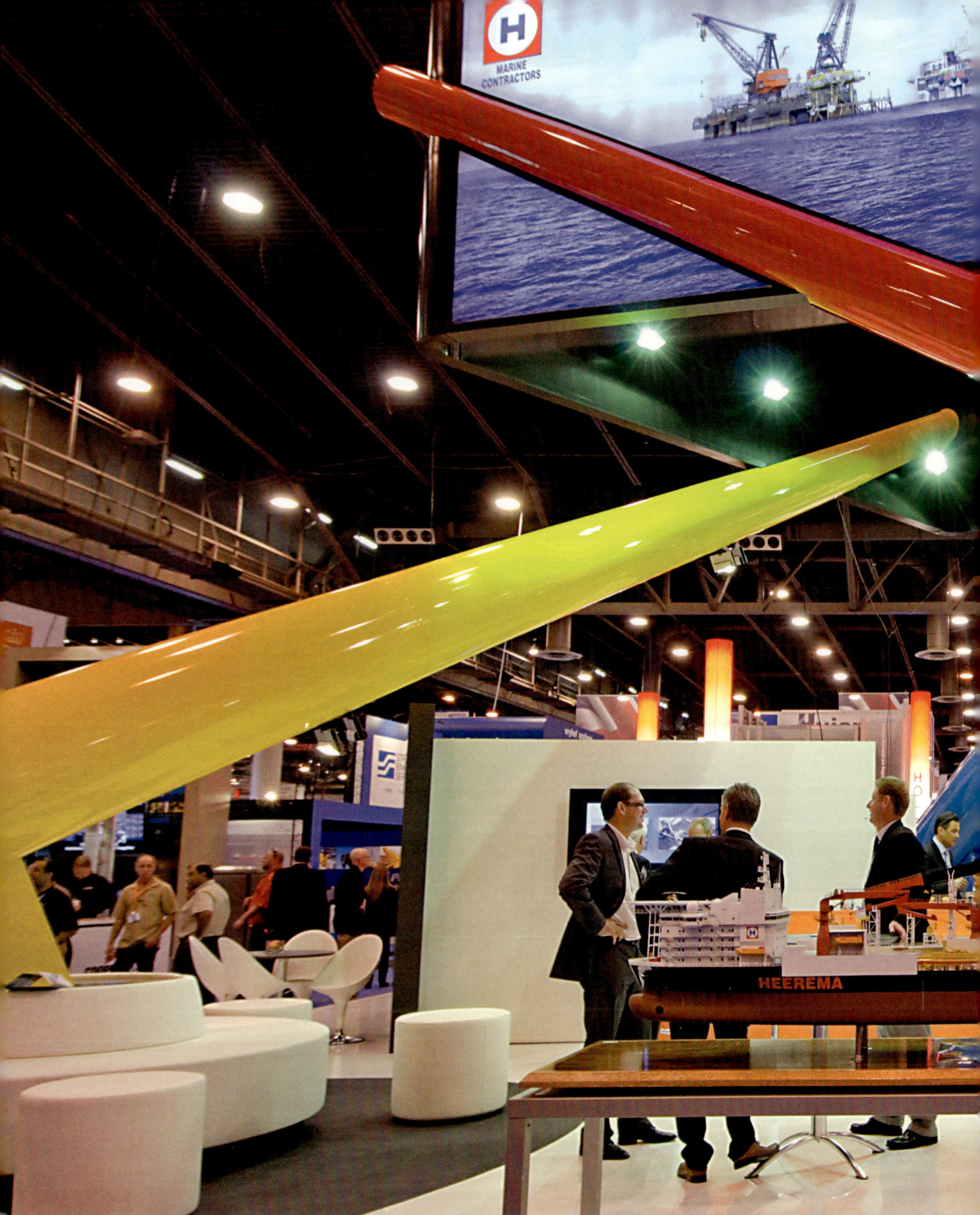

CORPORATE DESTINATION | The Offshore Technology Conference (OTC) is held at Reliant Park and represents the world's most noteworthy forum for the development of offshore resources. With annual participation by more than 2,000 companies and attendance of more than 50,000 people from around the globe, the OTC ranks as one of the Top 200 largest trade shows in the United States.

INTERNATIONAL CONVENTION | Held annually during the first week of May, the Offshore Technology Conference is one of the city's largest annual conventions and includes attendees from around the globe with more than 110 countries represented.

MARVELOUS MUSEUMS The Houston Museum District is one of the city's most cherished treasures. With 18 cultural centers and institutions of learning within a 1.5-mile radius, the district includes the world-renowned Museum of Fine Arts, Houston, and the Houston Museum of Natural Science with its beautiful grounds and Cockrell Butterfly Center.

Ageless Attractions

The Houston Museum of Natural Science ranks as one of the top four most heavily attended museums in the United States. Celebrating more than 100 years in Houston, this exceptional institution features a permanent collection that includes the Cullen Hall of Gems and Minerals, the Farish Hall of Texas Wildlife and the Alfred C. Glassell Jr. Hall of Paleontology.

ART HISTORY Established in 1900, the Museum of Fine Arts, Houston, is one of the largest in the United States and the oldest art museum in Texas. A visit to the museum offers distinguished collections and traveling exhibits throughout the year that attract thousands of visitors with stunning installments.

Learning Centers

The Houston Museum District is filled with exploration and discovery, from the biological wonders of the Cockrell Butterfly Center to the historical lessons of the dangers of prejudice and hatred at the Holocaust Museum Houston. Other favorite museums are the contemporary offerings of the Menil Collection and the Contemporary Arts Museum.

Honorary Arts — Located in River Oaks, the Bayou Bend Collection and Gardens is a facility of the Museum of Fine Arts, Houston. Opened to the public in 1966, Bayou Bend is the former home of Houston philanthropist Ima Hogg whose lush gardens complement without transforming the bayou she loved.

Animalistic Curiosity

With more than 1.5 million visitors a year, the Houston Zoo in the popular Hermann Park is the seventh most visited zoo in the country. It is home to more than 6,000 animals and is used for a variety of events for families and companies alike.

Natural Exploration

Located in Memorial Park, the Houston Arboretum and Nature Center is open daily with free admission. The park features more than five miles of nature trails, with forest, pond, wetland and meadow habitats as well as specialty gardens. Children are allowed to interact with nature throughout the year in age-appropriate classes and during special events around the holidays.

LIVING HISTORY

A 23,000-acre working ranch, George Ranch Historical Park aims to educate people of all ages about Texas history. At events throughout the year, George Ranch showcases reenactments of Texas conflicts and presents examples of soldier and civilian life from different historical eras. Family-run for four generations, it is one of Fort Bend County's most storied landmarks.

Performance Magic | The Hobby Center for the Performing Arts is Houston's premier venue for musical theater and other events. Every season, Broadway Across America brings to the stage new and classic musical productions that rival those of Broadway. Before or after a show, the Artista restaurant inside the center provides a great dining treat.

THEATRICAL HAVENS | Jones Hall for the Performing Arts is home to the Houston Symphony and the Houston Society for the Performing Arts. Down the street is the Wortham Theater Center, funded entirely by the private sector. Host to many of the world's most accomplished entertainers, it houses the Houston Ballet and Houston Grand Opera.

IMAGINE HOUSTON

DRAMATIC BEST | The Houston Theater District ranks second in the country in number of seats in a concentrated downtown area. The Alley Theatre's two stages showcase a wide-ranging repertoire of 11 productions each season with an emphasis on new American works. Just north of Houston in The Woodlands, the Cynthia Woods Mitchell Pavilion is an outdoor amphitheater supporting the region's major theatrical companies.

BAYOU BONANZA During 2011, Bayou Place in the theater district underwent major renovations, including the addition of the new Sundance Cinemas and Live! At Bayou Place on the second level with club venues including PBR Houston, Lucie's Liquors, Shark Bar and Chapel Spirits.

SOCIAL SCENE

One of Houston's many surprises is its thriving social and culinary world devoted to great times and good food. Anvil Bar & Refuge and Red Room make spirit-forward signature cocktails from fresh and often local ingredients while the simple French fare of Brasserie 19 and the tasty, organic food at Ruggles Green offer enticing treats for the taste buds in the Bayou City.

Unique Venues

In addition to large conventional event venues, Houston also is a hotbed for unique indoor and outdoor event spaces, including the historic Rice Hotel and the Houston Zoo in Hermann Park.

IMAGINE HOUSTON

SHOPPERS' PARADISE — With indoor and outdoor malls, free-standing boutiques and unique merchant centers in every major corner of the city, residents have access to myriad shopping destinations that include the most popular retail chains in the country. New additions include CityCentre and the Houston Pavilions while traditional favorites like the quaint streets of Old Town Spring continue to flourish.

MALL MIXTURE Shopping malls throughout the city vary in size and demographic. Suburban Sugar Land boasts the indoor-outdoor First Colony Mall. The Uptown Park Shopping Center offers countless opportunities to dine and shop. The Memorial City Mall provides more than just shopping with its NHL-sized indoor ice rink, which daily offers public skating.

FOOTBALL FANATICS | Houston is home to a longstanding tradition of sporting excellence. The NFL is represented by the Houston Texans, who have called Reliant Stadium home since their inception in 2002. The stadium has a seating capacity of 71,500 and was the first official NFL facility to have a retractable roof.

Indoor Baseball   America's favorite pastime has entertained Houston since 1962. The Houston Astros and their fans can be found downtown at Minute Maid Park. The indoor ballpark features a genuine grass field and a retractable roof, and it was the first major sports facility to have a closed-captioning board for the hearing impaired.

Sports Center

Professional hockey has a proud presence in Houston with the Houston Aeros, part of the American Hockey League. Since 1994, the Aeros have fought their way to three championship titles, playing their home games at the downtown Toyota Center, which the team shares with basketball's Houston Rockets. The modular indoor arena seats up to 18,300 people in 2,900 club seats and 103 luxury suites.

Soccer Stars — The Houston Dynamo represent the city in Major League Soccer (MLS). Since its start in 2005, the team has won the MLS Cup twice and qualified for playoffs almost every other year. Thus far sharing University of Houston's Robertson Stadium, the Dynamo will start the 2012 season at their brand-new soccer-specific open-air stadium that seats 22,000, the first of its kind in a major city's downtown district.

IMAGINE HOUSTON

URBAN UNIVERSITIES

Houston hosts a nationally recognized system of higher learning institutions. Baylor College of Medicine, located in the Texas Medical Center at the Roy and Lillie Cullen Building, currently ranks in the nation's Top 25 medical schools for research by *U.S. News & World Report* and has affiliations with eight teaching hospitals. The University of Houston-Downtown produces more than 2,000 graduates each year with degrees in the humanities, social sciences, business, technology and criminal justice.

HIGHER EDUCATION | Houston has some of the best higher education institutions in the region. The largest, University of Houston, offers more than 100 undergraduate majors and minors and nearly 200 graduate degree programs, some nationally ranked. The College of Optometry at the University of Houston offers students the opportunity to gain hands-on experience in their desired field.

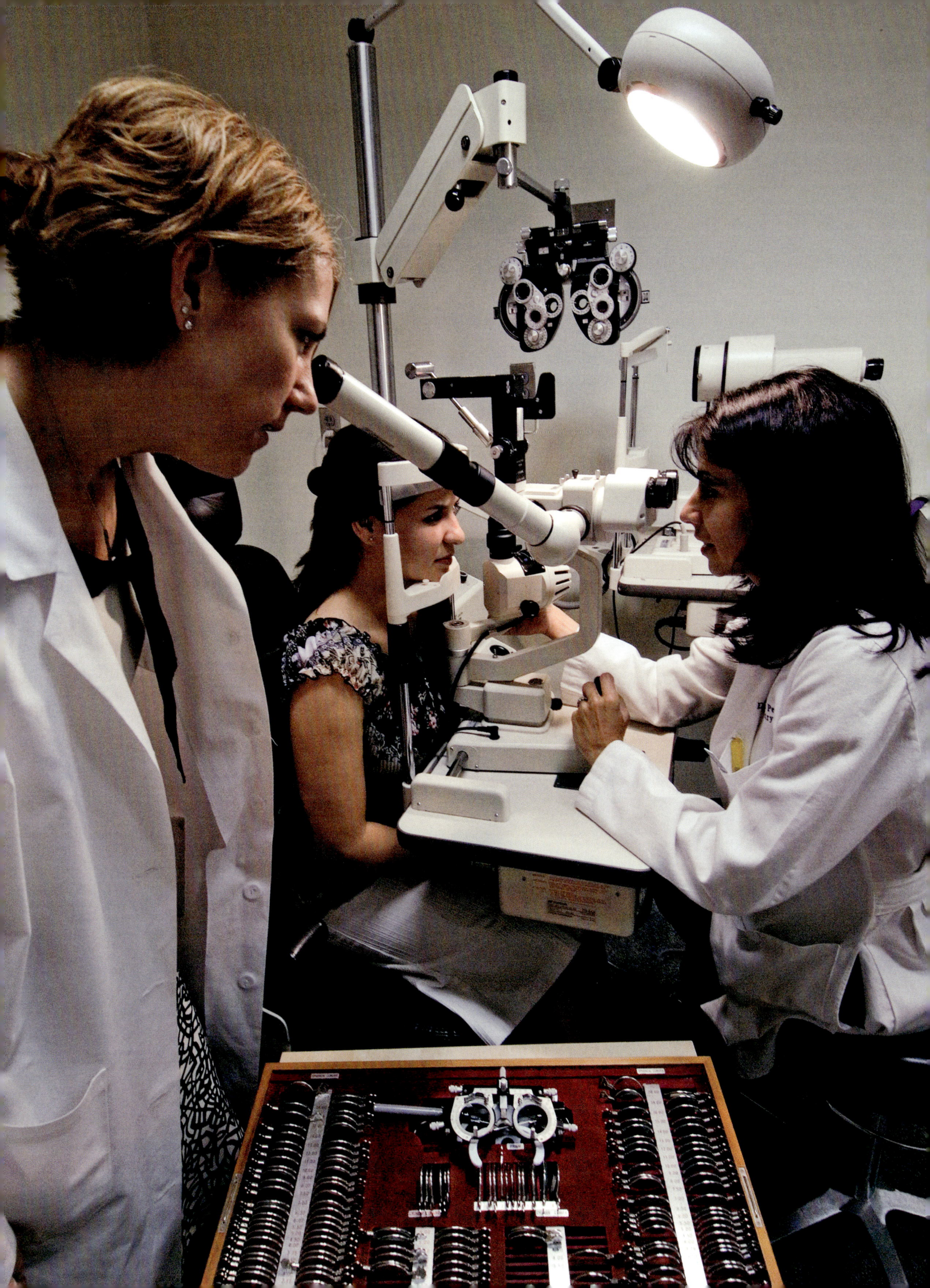

IVY LEAGUE SOUTH | Rice University consistently is ranked as one of the best learning and research institutions in the country. Rice provides students with excellent faculty and rigorous academic curricula, which results in highly reputable degrees, postcollegiate success and opportunity for scholarly advancement. Encouraging diversity, Rice University's international and transnational student body comprises degree candidates from more than 89 countries and all 50 states.

EDUCATIONAL VARIETY

Houston boasts various smaller universities with stellar qualities. The University of St. Thomas in the Museum District provides a low student-to-faculty ratio. Houston Baptist University has developed a flourishing community of faith and scholarship since 1960. Prairie View A&M University is the second oldest public university in Texas with three campuses. Downtown's South Texas College of Law is Houston's oldest law school and offers far-reaching study abroad programs.

Educational Opportunities

Those in the Houston area seeking higher education certainly have options. Texas Southern University is one of the nation's largest historically black universities and offers programs in nine different schools and colleges. Established in 1891, the University of Texas Medical Branch at Galveston encompasses four schools and seven hospitals. The Houston Community College system offers terminal degrees, certificates and transfer credits at six different campuses throughout the city.

HEALTH CARE HEARTLAND | The Texas Medical Center comprises 49 nonprofit institutions, including 13 renowned hospitals, two specialty institutions, two medical schools, four nursing schools and schools in virtually all health-related fields. People from every social circumstance and many nations worldwide seek treatment and find sanctuary in this world-renowned medical community.

PATIENT PRIORITY | Texas Children's Hospital is an internationally recognized pediatric facility, ranked nationally in 10 specialties by *U.S. News & World Report*. In addition, Memorial Hermann, the largest not-for-profit healthcare system in Texas, serves the greater Houston community through 11 hospitals, a vast network of affiliated physicians and numerous specialty programs and services.

Reassuring Services

The Texas Medical Center has a reputation for outstanding service and care. The area surrounding the Texas Medical Center is a hub of activity with tranquil pedestrian areas and facilities for employees and their children, patients and tourists visiting the region.

SPECIALIZED FOCUS | The Methodist Hospital Research Institute is a nationally recognized nonprofit organization affiliated with the Texas Annual Conference of the United Methodist Church. It has a network of community-based hospitals focused on research, education, training and pioneering advancements. Shriners Hospital for Children focuses on the well-being of children, including orthopedic care, burn care, spinal cord rehabilitation, cleft lip and palate care and continuing pediatric research and education.

LEADING FACILITIES — The University of Texas MD Anderson Cancer Center is dedicated to eliminating cancer through research and prevention programs. *U.S. News & World Report* has ranked MD Anderson as the top hospital in the nation for cancer care for seven of the past nine years. More than 96,000 people seek quality care from MD Anderson each year.

Personalized Care

St. Luke's Episcopal Health System is a faith-based, nonprofit organization that approaches medical healing with a team of professionals that provide top-rate medical care with a human touch. The Kelsey-Seybold Clinic provides primary and specialty care at 20 clinics throughout Houston for more than 400,000 patients each year, including members of NASA. Opened in 2010, the Methodist Hospital Outpatient Center is Texas' largest facility solely dedicated to patient care.

SKYWARD BOUND

The Houston Airport System is the sixth largest in the world with its three airports: William P. Hobby Airport, Ellington International Airport and George Bush Intercontinental Airport (IAH). Houston's largest airport, IAH supports more than 700 daily departures by 17 passenger airlines and is the seventh busiest airport in the United States for total passenger traffic, featuring five passenger terminals, more than 880,000 square feet of cargo area and a consolidated car rental facility.

TRANSPORTATION TRENDS

Due to the city's expansive layout, personal transportation still plays a major role in the lives of most Houstonians. However, residents living and working inside the Inner Loop have several eco-friendly alternatives, such as the electric REV Eco-Shuttle, group bus charters for corporate events and the METRO public transportation system of buses and trains.

TRADE GIANT | The Fred Hartman Bridge above the Houston Ship Channel connects Baytown and La Porte just west of Houston. The shipping channel continues to be a vital trade artery in the region, sustaining businesses that facilitate 785,000 Texas jobs and generate $118 million on a state level. Englewood Yard is Houston's busy Union Pacific Railroad hump yard, which keeps Houston connected and its cargo moving in and out of the city from coast to coast.

ENERGY CENTRAL | Houston remains the Energy Capital of the World not only because of the abundance of resources found in the region, but also because of the density of national corporations headquartered in the city. With local teams of geologists and geophysicists developing new techniques for fossil fuel extraction and discovery, the strength of the local industry shows no sign of slowing down.

OFFSHORE RESOURCES | The Gulf Coast Region of Texas has long been established as the center for offshore drilling. Several international corporations, such as ConocoPhillips, Chevron and BP, have a significant presence in local oil and gas development and operations.

Photography

Photography Credit

All photos by Publishing Resources, Charles Edwards, except for: **Port of Houston Authority:** 72, 76 **Houston Texans:** 142, 143 **Houston Astros:** 144, 145 (bottom) **Houston Aeros:** 146 **Houston Dynamo:** 148 **Apache Corporation:** 178 **Chevron:** 179 (top) **GlobalSantaFe Corporation:** 179 (bottom) **BP America:** 180

Brilliant Ballet | Located in the heart of downtown in Houston's Theater District, the Houston Ballet's Center for Dance is a six-story, 115,000-square-foot facility with sustainable architecture. The building features nine dance studios, a dance lab for presentations and rehearsals that seats 175 and administrative offices for the Houston Ballet and its academy.

HOUSTON
MOST SUCCESSFUL 2012 PROFILES

ACCOUNTANTS
Ernst & Young 186

ATTORNEYS
Osha Liang LLP 189
The Voss Law Firm, P.C. 187
Vernier & Barry, P.C. 188

AUTO DEALERS
Auto World of Texas 190

CHARITIES, NOT-FOR-PROFITS
YMCA of Greater Houston 191

CHURCHES
Houston's First Baptist Church 192

COLLEGES AND UNIVERSITIES
Houston Community College 193
University of Houston – C.T. Bauer College of Business 194

COMMERCIAL REALTORS
GSL Welcome Group 195

DENTISTS
Carrick Dentistry 196
Terri Alani, DDS 197

EMERGENCY CARE CENTERS
River Oaks Emergency Center 199
Texas Emergency Care Center 198

HOMEBUILDERS
Chesmar Homes 202
Del Webb Sweetgrass 200
Trendmaker Homes 203

INSURANCE COMPANIES
Insgroup, Inc. 204
Nationwide Insurance – The May Group LLC 205

MASTER-PLANNED COMMUNITIES
Caldwell Companies 206
Cross Creek Ranch 209
Firethorne 208
Silver Ranch 210
Towne Lake 207

NEIGHBORHOODS AND CITIES
City of Nassau Bay 211

OIL & GAS – EQUIPMENT & SERVICES
Cameron 212
FMC Technologies 214
Key Energy Services, Inc. 216
Schlumberger Oilfield Services 217

OIL & GAS – EXPLORATION
Chevron 220
CITGO Petroleum Corporation 218

PHYSICIANS
Orthopaedic Associates, L.L.P. 221

PORTS
Port of Galveston 222

REALTORS
RE/MAX 360 224
The David Young Team 225
The Gretzer Group 223

WEALTH MANAGEMENT COMPANIES
ZT Wealth 226

ACCOUNTANTS

ERNST & YOUNG

OFFERING DEEP INDUSTRY EXPERIENCE TO HELP COMPANIES SUCCEED IN A COMPLEX ENVIRONMENT

Charles Swanson, Houston Office Managing Partner, works closely with Marcela Donadio, Americas Oil & Gas Sector Leader, in serving the needs of the energy industry.

ERNST & YOUNG
Quality In Everything We Do

Visit the Ernst & Young
Energy Center at:
1401 McKinney Street, 15th Floor
Houston, Texas 77010
(713) 750-1388
www.ey.com/us/oilandgas

Energy companies are working hard to meet demand, braving new frontiers for exploration and production while developing technologies to tap challenging reservoirs and unconventional fuel sources. And they're doing it in an environment where resources are constrained and government policies are in flux. With more than 1,500 energy audit, tax, transaction, and advisory professionals in the US alone, the Ernst & Young Oil & Gas Center in Houston is poised and ready to respond to the pressures and problems energy companies face.

"Ernst & Young energy professionals are located in key oil and gas producing markets throughout the globe with extensive audit, advisory, tax and transaction experience to provide well-informed practical advice to our clients," said Charles Swanson, Houston Office Managing Partner.

WHAT WE DO
Assurance: Ernst &Young's risk-based approach to audit services focuses on the drivers of the business, the associated risks and their potential effects on financial statements.

Advisory: Our performance improvement services are focused on finance, supply chain operations, and customer management. Ernst &Young helps clients mitigate risk in financial and operational areas of energy companies.

Tax: Our integrated global network is comprised of dedicated international tax professionals who work together to help clients uncover opportunities, manage global tax risks, meet cross-border reporting obligations, deal with transfer pricing issues and the demands of tax filing in multiple jurisdictions.

Transactions: Ernst & Young provides financial, tax, technology, operational, commercial and legal due-diligence assistance for energy companies involved in mergers and acquisitions. Post-deal, we provide integration support.

HOW WE DO IT
The Oil & Gas Center works with some of the world's largest integrated energy companies, as well as many of the largest independent exploration and production, oilfield services and refining and marketing companies. "Our clients benefit from our knowledge and experience working with a variety of energy companies," said Americas Oil and Gas Sector Leader, Marcela Donadio. "We've seen different scenarios played out, lived the implementations and experienced the results. As a result, we're providing tried and true counsel to our clients." ■

THE VOSS LAW FIRM

A WORLD-CLASS ATTORNEY WITH A TEXAS HEART

The Voss Law Firm, P.C.
The Voss Law Center
26619 Interstate 45 North
The Woodlands, Texas 77380

Phone: (281) VICTORY
Toll free: (866) 276-6179
Fax: (713) 861-0021
www.vosslawfirm.com

Attorney Bill Voss is a ninth-generation Texan who serves individuals and business owners around the country, helping them resolve their disputes with the passion his clients deserve. He has been recognized in local and national publications, such as the *Legal News*, *Forbes*, *Newsweek*, *Inc.*, *Texas Monthly*, *H Texas* and the *Houston Press*. He recently was named a "Rising Star" by his peers in *Super Lawyers*, one of Houston's "Top Lawyers for the People" in *H Texas* and a "Top Attorney in the Country" by *Newsweek*.

Attorney Bill Voss has recruited the nation's top attorneys to work together with expertise in areas of commercial and business litigation, business law, insurance litigation, wrongful death litigation, offshore injuries, catastrophic personal injury litigation, employment litigation, oil and gas law, consumer fraud, rare coin fraud and first-party insurance claims.

Attorney Bill Voss is passionate about the law and helping the proverbial little guy. "I truly enjoy what I do, bringing wrongdoers to justice and helping clients, especially in those 'gorilla-type' cases." Hard work and tenacity are attributes that helped Voss achieve success not only in trial, but also in life, and these qualities are ones he impresses on the attorneys and staff of The Voss Law Firm. "We have an outstanding track record of success here. We have the resources and experience to handle the largest, most complex cases. Clients and referring attorneys can be assured that we do not back down in the face of adversity. The tougher and bigger the opposition, the better for our law firm; we get completely fired up for a good legal battle. Those are the type of employees that I have assembled here—ones that are going to fight hard for our clients. We wouldn't have it any other way."

The Voss Law Firm, P.C. proudly serves all Texas counties and cities including but not limited to the following: Harris County, Montgomery County, Jefferson County, Houston, The Woodlands, Beaumont, El Paso, San Antonio, Austin, Sugar Land, Dallas, Fort Worth, Orange and Port Arthur, as well as companies and individuals along the Gulf Coast and around the globe. ■

ATTORNEYS

VERNIER & BARRY, P.C.
EXPERIENCE • EXPERTISE • ZEALOUS REPRESENTATION

Vernier & Barry, P.C.

2441 High Timbers Drive, Suite 110
The Woodlands, Texas 77380
(281) 364-1187
www.vernierlawfirm.com

At Vernier & Barry, P.C., our focus is family law, which allows us to respond quickly and expertly to any family matter. We offer expert representation in any family law matter, from divorce to international child abduction. Our extensive experience in family law provides us with the necessary legal expertise to achieve our clients' objectives. It gives us a clear understanding of family matters so that we can address the needs of our clients with commitment and skill, as well as sensitivity and compassion. Every member of our firm is very familiar with family law matters and is dedicated to serving our clients with great competence and sensitivity.

Named Top Lawyer five of the last six years, Attorney Ruth Vernier possesses the needed experience and expertise in all aspects of the law affecting families. Her willingness to be a strong supporter of the community and her firm belief in helping families in their time of need allows her to bring out the human element with each family she works with. It is with this foundation that she approaches each case with a thorough understanding of the law and a strict eye for detail. The firm has the resources to skillfully handle the most complex family matters.

The firm has built a powerful network of expert accountants, appraisers, investigators, mental health professionals, and other experts specializing in domestic matters.

At Vernier & Barry, P.C., we are both results – and people-oriented. We match experience and expertise with strong and personal support to help you through even the most complex and difficult family matter.

Family is our focus. Your Family is a Priority ■

ATTORNEYS

OSHA LIANG LLP

INTELLECTUAL PROPERTY LAW

OSHALiANG
Intellectual Property Law

909 Fannin, Suite 3500
Houston, Texas 77010
(713) 228-8600
www.oshaliang.com

Founded in Houston in 1998, Osha Liang LLP is a full-service intellectual property law firm with a global presence. With offices in Texas, California, France, and Japan, the firm specializes in protecting and enforcing intellectual property interests on a world-wide basis.

Osha Liang's expertise spans the gamut from international patent and trademark procurement to litigation and strategic IP counseling. The firm is frequently recognized as a leading IP firm, and has been included in *IP Today* magazine's list of top 50 IP firms in the U.S. (based on the number of issued utility patents) for the past four years.

Through strictly organic growth, the firm has increased in size from the original team of 13 members in 1998 to more than 120 employees today. Osha Liang is proud to be one of the largest IP boutiques in the Gulf Coast region. The firm has twice been named to *The Houston Business Journal's* "Fast 100" list of fastest growing companies.

One of the many forward-looking aspects of the firm's practice is the Patent Agent program. Osha Liang recruits science and engineering graduates from universities and industry who are then apprenticed in patent practice through on-the-job training and weekly lectures. Eventually, Patent Engineers are encouraged to sit for the United States Patent and Trademark Office registration exam to become licensed Patent Agents. Patent Agents then have the option to attend law school with tuition assistance provided by the firm. ∎

AUTO DEALERS

AUTO WORLD OF TEXAS

LUXURY, DOMESTIC, AND PERFORMANCE BRANDS THAT REFLECT OF YOUR PERSONAL TASTE AND SUCCESS

AUTO WORLD OF TEXAS
3233 West 11th Street
Houston, Texas 77008
(713) 880-1902
(713) 298-5784
www.autoworldoftexas.net

Are you ready for a night on the town in your new car? We can help you today! At Auto World of Texas we carry the best hand picked selection of luxury, domestic, and performance brands at significant savings. You can drive a reflection of your personal taste and success for less!

We have a pre-purchase inspection policy. This means you personally check out your car before you put your name on the bottom line. This way you don't have any surprise problems after the car is sold and it saves you time and money.

We know your time is valuable. Let us locate your next automobile purchase. Our proven accomplishments demonstrate that we've saved customers an average of 15 percent to 35 percent of their hard earned money.

You will receive an experience like no other when you come to Auto World of Texas. Here you will find the best trained and educated automobile consultants in the business. Selling over 100 vehicles a month, we know what it means to purchase a vehicle. We understand that next to your home, purchasing a vehicle is one of the most expensive purchases you will make. We have changed the industry so that you can have a choice when it comes to making your purchase. If you are ready for a revolutionary car-buying experience, come by and give us a chance.

With over 10 years serving the Great Houston Area, we know how to take care of our customers – before, during, and after the sale. Whether you need a foreign or domestic car for yourself or as the perfect gift for a friend, Auto World of Texas will make it happen.

CHARITIES, NOT-FOR-PROFITS

YMCA OF GREATER HOUSTON

NOT JUST A HEALTHY LIFE, BUT A BETTER LIFE

YMCA of Greater Houston
(713) 659-5566
www.ymcahouston.org

The YMCA of Greater Houston is committed to putting Christian principles into practice. YMCA programs, activities and relationships teach and model Judeo-Christian values in order to strengthen kids, families and communities through programs that build healthy spirit, mind and body for all. Caring, honesty, respect, responsibility and faith are core values evident in all that we do.

Strengthening community is our goal at the YMCA. Every day, we work side-by-side with our neighbors to make sure that everyone, regardless of age, income or background, has the opportunity to learn, grow and thrive. We are committed to strengthening communities through youth development, healthy living and social responsibility.

At the Y, we provide the necessary support and opportunities that empower people and communities. With a focus on youth development, healthy living and social responsibility, the Y nurtures the potential of every youth and teen, improves the community's health and well-being and provides opportunities to give back and support our neighbors.

We have the presence and partnerships to not just promise, but to deliver, lasting personal and social change. For more than 125 years, we've been listening and responding to the Houston community. We connect people of all ages and backgrounds to bridge the gaps in community needs and mobilize local communities to effect meaningful change.

The YMCA of Greater Houston is dedicated to building healthy, confident, connected children, adults, families and communities. Every day our impact is felt when an individual makes a healthy choice, when a mentor inspires a child and when a community comes together for the common good. ∎

CHURCHES

HOUSTON'S FIRST BAPTIST CHURCH

KEEPING THE FAITH AND GROWING STRONG

HOUSTON'S FIRST
BAPTIST CHURCH

7401 Katy Freeway
Houston, Texas 77024
(713) 681-8000
www.HoustonsFirst.org

On the muddy banks of Buffalo Bayou in 1841—five years after Texas won independence from Mexico—16 men and women united to organize Houston's First Baptist Church. Throughout its history, the church has survived wars, yellow fever epidemics, financial hardship and the 1900 Galveston hurricane that destroyed one of its early buildings.

Along the way, the church faithfully gave back to its hometown. Church leaders established Star of Hope Mission, and a clinic that today is Memorial Hermann Healthcare System. Sunday School classes created for the community later became churches themselves, including Chinese Baptist Church and Woodhaven Baptist Deaf Church.

In 1977, under the leadership of Dr. John Bisagno, a renewed emphasis on evangelism, strong religious education and a vision for missions sparked phenomenal growth in the old church, requiring Houston's First to relocate from its longtime downtown location to a larger home at I-10 (Katy Freeway) and West 610 Loop.

Pastor Gregg Matte became the Pastor of Houston's First in 2004. While studying at Texas A&M University, Pastor Gregg founded Breakaway Ministries, the nation's largest on-campus college Bible study.

Pastor Gregg is the author of *Finding God's Will* and *I AM Changes Who i am*, and in 2011, he received the Outstanding Alumni Award from the Texas A&M Mays Business School.

Houston's First continues to serve the community through programs and ministries far beyond Sunday mornings. A fitness and recreation center and counseling center offer services for church members and guests. First Baptist Academy provides college-preparatory education for early childhood through eighth grade. The church's Faith Center sponsors ministries such as a food pantry, clothes closet, ESL classes and afterschool programs.

In 2011, Houston's First returned to its roots, opening a downtown campus at 1010 Lamar where the church gathered for decades. Located in the underground pedestrian tunnel system, the downtown campus provides a convenient church home for downtown residents and those along the METRORail.

Houston has changed tremendously since the church's 1841 founding, and Houston's First continues to provide a relevant biblical community. The church invites longtime Houstonians and first-time guests to visit on Sundays or anytime. ∎

COLLEGES AND UNIVERSITIES

HOUSTON COMMUNITY COLLEGE

HCC IS A GATEWAY TO EDUCATION, TO JOBS AND TO THE FUTURE

HOUSTON COMMUNITY COLLEGE

3100 Main Street
Houston, Texas 77002
(713) 718-2000
www.hccs.edu

It is no accident that more and more students are turning to Houston Community College for an education, training and hope for the future. HCC is giving people opportunity to grow through education.

It is true that in difficult economies people turn to higher education, but they are coming to us in extraordinary numbers. Our growth trajectory is remarkable with more than a 30% increase in just the last two years. Today, we are educating more than 75,000 students each semester, on our way to 80,000 this term. While this is impressive, more impressive is our comparison to other community colleges in the state, which averaged an 18% increase. Our dual enrollment/high school students now top 6,500 and on-line students exceed 17,000.

And we are handling enrollments more efficiently as evidenced by the number of sections at capacity as of fall census – from the 11% in 2009 to 43% this semester while keeping average class sizes small, at 22 to 1.....the result of team work by administrators and faculty as we do more with less!

Financial aid has helped ease the cost of attendance by increasing dramatically from $50 million in the 2008 academic year to $119 million dollars disbursed for the 2010 academic year, representing a 131% increase.

We introduced two innovations for the 2010 – 2011 academic year, examples of why students are choosing HCC: renting textbooks to reduce costs by 40% and offering on-campus living options through a partnership with the University of Houston.

And we are not just bringing new students in the front door….we are retaining them too. The new magic word is COMPLETION – course completion, college completion, completion by design, completion to degree, time to completion – you get the idea! Our Achieving the Dream outcomes have received national recognition. 74.8% of first-time students persisted from Fall 2008 to Spring 2009, a dramatic improvement from the 68.2% from Fall 2001 to Spring 2002. Thanks to our dedicated faculty and staff, strategies implemented and research conducted through Houston Endowment and Lumina and Gates foundation funds, over the last two years we have kept more than 1,400 students in school who otherwise would have left. Named as one of 15 national Leader Colleges, we are moving the needle at the developmental education level. And our transfer rate has increased to 40.5%.

With one of the largest and most diverse student bodies in the country, our Associate Degree graduates earn an average of $59,700 annually, 35% more than students with a high school diploma. They enjoy a 14.9% average rate of return on their HCC investment. And those who are no longer attending HCC continue to contribute to the regional economy while students who come from outside our area bring in an additional $102.6 million annually to our economy.

We are always looking to strengthen and grow our offerings to meet the community's needs – through new academic courses and innovative career programs. Twenty-five of our workforce programs are recognized as exemplary by the state of Texas, more than any other community college in the state. Our graduates are prepared to work and contribute immediately. ■

| Advertorial |

COLLEGES AND UNIVERSITIES

UNIVERSITY OF HOUSTON C.T. BAUER COLLEGE OF BUSINESS

HOUSTON'S TOP BUSINESS SCHOOL FOR THE REAL WORLD OF BUSINESS

Left: The University of Houston C.T. Bauer College of Business is home to The Cyvia and Melvyn Wolff Center for Entrepreneurship, the #1 ranked program in the nation according to The Princeton Review and Entrepreneur magazine. **Right:** Whether pursuing an undergraduate, MBA, MS in Finance or Accounting, or doctoral degree, many come from all over the world to study at UH Bauer, Houston's most comprehensive business school.

UNIVERSITY of HOUSTON
C. T. BAUER COLLEGE of BUSINESS

334 Melcher Hall
Houston, Texas 77204
(713) 743-4600
www.bauer.uh.edu

The C. T. Bauer College of Business at the University of Houston is at the heart of the city's vibrant, sophisticated, international business universe. Bauer College is powered by the energy of Houston.

Top ranked programs in entrepreneurship and energy reflect the innovative flair of this global energy capital.

The accounting and sales excellence programs show how close ties to Houston's business community enrich programs and create job opportunities for students.

Bauer's Global Energy Management Institute is a training ground for energy leaders in Houston and the world.

The college is also known for the hands-on experiences for students and the energy of its faculty, which ranks among top colleges for its output and insight of its research.

Over the past 10 years, Bauer has grown in size and the breadth of its programs. Bauer recently expanded with Michael J. Cemo Hall, which houses added classrooms and the Rockwell Career Center. With more senior executives earning degrees from Bauer than any other school in Houston, Bauer alumni lead the real world of business.

Bauer is Houston's most comprehensive business school and fully accredited by the Association to Advance Collegiate Schools of Business (AACSB). Bauer offers BBA, MBA, M.S., MPA and Ph.D. programs as well special certificates at the graduate level in energy, real estate, entrepreneurship, leadership, marketing and supply chain.

BBAs are offered in Accounting, Finance, Management, Marketing, Entrepreneurship, Management Information Systems and Supply Chain Management.

Bauer has a strong reputation and is one of the most diverse business schools in the nation. The school boasts many top rankings, including the Wolff Center for Entrepreneurship's #1 ranking in the U.S. (Best 2011 Entrepreneurial Colleges, The Princeton Review); a part-time MBA program ranked in the top 30 in the nation among 127 schools of business at public universities (U.S. News & World Report); marketing and finance faculty ranked in the top 10 in the U.S.; and an accountancy & taxation program that is one of only 17 worldwide designated a Partner of the Institute of Internal Auditors.

Learn more about UH Bauer College at **bauer.uh.edu**.

COMMERCIAL REALTORS

GSL Welcome Group

ONE-STOP-SHOP FOR REAL ESTATE DEVELOPMENT

Welcome Group, LLC

5858 Westheimer, Suite 800
Houston, Texas 77057
(713) 952-7000
www.gslwelcome.com

Welcome Group, parent company of GSL Welcome Group, owns and leases single-tenant industrial, laboratory, office and manufacturing facilities.

Welcome Group principals are Welcome Wilson, Sr., Welcome Wilson, Jr., and Craig G. Wilson. We are unique in the market as a one-stop-shop real estate development group, which will handle land acquisition, construction financing, development, design and construction, management and permanent financing.

We work closely with our design construction affiliate, Kingham Dalton Wilson, Ltd. to offer build-to-suit and design/build services for new projects. Welcome Group, and its predecessor, has developed more than 180 single-tenant properties.

Our clients include many Fortune 500 Companies as well as regional, local and a number of international companies.

In addition to build-to-suit and design/build projects, we seek to purchase existing occupied single-tenant commercial properties.

Welcome Group currently owns more than 75 facilities comprising approximately 3.5 million square feet. We were ranked the No.10 Largest Commercial Property Owner in Houston by *Houston Business Journal* in 2010.

The Wilson family are original Texans with roots dating back to before Texas was a state. We are committed to the future of Houston and Texas through our work on the University of Houston Board of Regents, Greater Houston Partnership, Houston Food Bank and many other community efforts. ∎

DENTISTS

CARRICK DENTISTRY

DENTISTRY WITH A SMILE

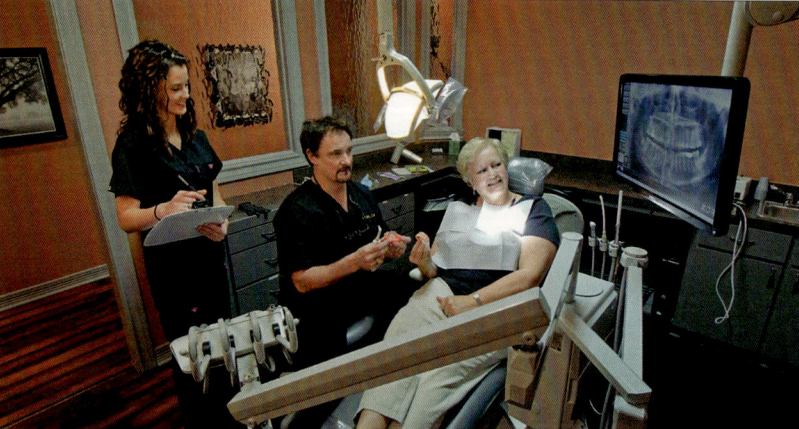
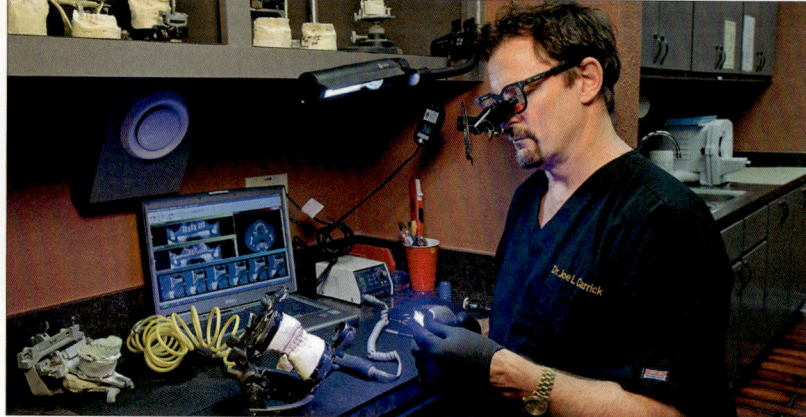

1805 West White Oak Terrace,
Suite D
Conroe, Texas 77304
(936) 828-0676
www.drjoecarrick.com

For 34 years, it has been Dr. Carrick's personal goal to provide his patients with the best possible care by building strong, trusting relationships. He spends extra time to realize a shared vision of excellence as well as provide a better quality of life for those dissatisfied with their smile.

Dr. Carrick's revolutionary concept of TOTAL DENTISTRY ensures a true, one-stop dental experience. While he specializes in full mouth restorations, he is fully certified and remains an industry leader in implants, endodontics, secure dentures, and cosmetic dentistry. He also provides the popular "oral sedation dentistry." In addition to Dr. Carrick's impressive specialized services you may also receive general dental procedures and dental cleanings.

Dr. Carrick teaches as an adjunct professor at several national and international universities. He also routinely writes articles, which are published in various dental journals. His qualifications, passion for his patients, and dedication to the concept of TOTAL DENTISTRY make him one-of-a-kind. ∎

DEGREES
B.S. with Honors at West Texas State University
D.D.S. at University of Texas, San Antonio

SPECIAL ACHIEVEMENTS
American Academy of Cosmetic Dentistry
  – Past President
A.A.C.D. – Accredited American Academy of Cosmetic Dentistry
F.A.A.C.D. – Fellow Status American Academy of Cosmetic Dentistry
A.A.C.D. Board of Directors
Fellow and Diplomat International Congress of Oral Implantology
Examiner for American Academy of Cosmetic Dentistry
Editor of the Journal of Cosmetic Dentistry
Adjunct Professor Postgraduate Studies U.T. Dental School San Antonio
Designed the ERA Implant and surgical protocol

AFFILIATIONS
The Woodlands Chamber of Commerce
One of Houston's Top Dentists
American Academy of Cosmetic Dentistry
International Congress of Oral Implantologists
Military Service: U.S. Navy, 1977-1980

Terri Alani DDS

A BEAUTIFUL SMILE SPEAKS WHEN YOU DON'T

A beautiful smile speaks when you don't. Dr. Terri Alani is an experienced and caring dentist with a mission to not only take care of her patients smiles, but to educate them on the importance of good oral health as it relates to ones overall health. How does this dental office stand out from others? Dr. Alani states, "We are a small office with an amazing amount of personalized care."

"Every staff member is trained to give each patient great service. We take blood pressure readings on every patient and provide oral cancer exams using new technology. Our treatment plans are customized based on the needs of each patient."

Dr. Alani is a general dentist, but her passion is cosmetic dentistry. Her cosmetic services include Zoom whitening, Snap on Smile, Invisalign, veneers, lumineers and metal free crowns.

Known as the TexasToothLady, Dr. Alani continues educating patients as a monthly regular on Channel 11's Great Day Houston for the past five years, as well as a panelist for Medical Mondays. She has been featured on Channel 13, Fox news and Channel 2.

Dr. Alani currently serves as the Chair of the Media Committee for The Greater Houston District Dental Society and also serves on the Advisory Council for the College of Science at Texas A&M. Radio also taps her nearly 30-year expertise as talk-show host with her brother, orthopedic surgeon, Dr. Wayne Alani. Together they discuss health-related topics every Saturday at 9 a.m. on CNN 650. She has been voted one of H-Magazines best dentist five times in the Houston area.

"Patients ask me when I am going to retire. I say never!! I absolutely love my job and the incredible fulfillment I get from knowing I have made a positive change in someone's life! We promise to give you our best efforts and a magnificent smile!"

Dr. Alani is on TV KHOU 11 Houston and on radio CNN650.

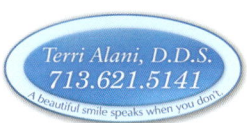

5636 Westheimer
Houston, Texas 77056
(713) 621-5141
www.texastoothlady.com

EMERGENCY CARE CENTERS

TEXAS EMERGENCY CARE CENTER

EXPERT EMERGENCY CARE NOW IN YOUR NEIGHBORHOOD

TEXAS EMERGENCY CARE CENTER
RAPID RESPONSE. EXPERT CARE.™

ATASCOCITA
19143 West Lake Houston Parkway
West Lake Houston Parkway
at FM 1960
(281) 540-9113

PEARLAND
3115 Dixie Farm Road, Suite 107
FM 518 at Dixie Farm Road
(281) 648-9113

CYPRESS
17255 Spring Cypress Road, Suite A
Spring Cypress at Skinner Road
(281) 304-9113

www.txercare.com

A Lincesed, Free-Standing
Emergency Medical Care Facility

When an emergency strikes getting expert care, quickly, is the first priority. Time is of the essence. You rush to the nearest emergency room, only to sit and wait. And wait. It could be hours before you see a physician. In some instances, your condition can worsen while you wait.

This is a common, and frustrating, experience shared by many emergency room visitors. Fortunately there is now a better way to get expert emergency care, close to home, as soon as you need it.

Texas Emergency Care Center is a licensed, free-standing emergency room that provides all the same services as a hospital-based emergency room but with minimal wait times, in a comfortable environment that's close to home. In fact, wait times at Texas Emergency Care Center average less than 20 minutes. And just like a hospital ER, Texas Emergency Care Center is open 24 hours a day, seven days a week, 365 days a year.

Equipped with the most up-to-date medical equipment including CT Scan, ultra sound, X-Ray and heart monitoring equipment, the specialists at Texas Emergency Care Center can treat everything from chest pain to broken bones. The physicians at Texas Emergency Care Center are experts. All physicians on staff are board certified or board eligible in emergency medicine and nurses are all specially trained in emergency medicine. The team coordinates care with patient's regular physicians, arranges hospital admittance if needed, and personally follows-up with patients after their emergency room visit.

For more information about Texas Emergency Care Center, visit **www.txercare.com**.

EMERGENCY CARE CENTERS

RIVER OAKS EMERGENCY CENTER

SPECIALIZING IN QUICK RESPONSE AND ACCURATE CARE

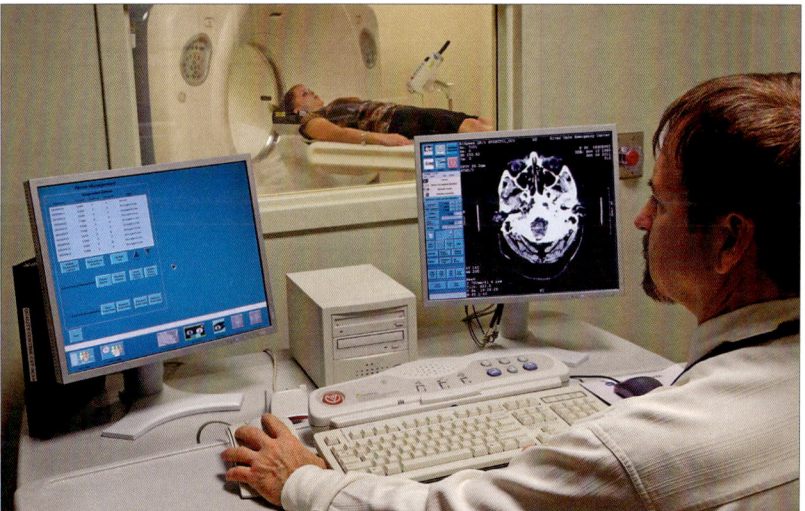

+ RIVER OAKS EMERGENCY CENTER
A Department of First Street Hospital

2320 South Shepherd Drive
Houston, Texas 77019
(713) 526-2320
www.riveroaksemergency.com

During an emergency every second counts. We are always ready to take care of your emergency. River Oaks Emergency Center gives you the trust and reliability in medical care for you and your loved ones.

At River Oaks Emergency Center, we are able to provide the highest quality emergency care through a freestanding emergency center. We are open twenty four hours a day, seven days a week with an average wait time of less than ten minutes, all while providing a high-level emergency care for urgent and life threatening emergency conditions.

River Oaks Emergency Center is committed to a growing health care customer-service movement that promotes quality and efficiency. Our Freestanding Emergency Center improves access to timely emergency medical care. We operate under the processes and protocols that are administratively linked to hospitals.

You can rest assured that upon arrival at River Oaks Emergency Center you will receive a prompt examination and will be treated by experienced and caring registered nurse and emergency room physicians. Immediate testing and diagnosis is available with River Oaks Emergency X-Ray, CT Scanning, Ultrasound and Laboratory. After receiving treatment you will be discharged home, or if needed you will be transferred to another facility with direct admission to a hospital.

For the comfort of our guests and family members, a lobby area and coffee bar are available while awaiting treatment. Our goal is to provide you with a comfortable, elegant and calm health care environment for both you and your family or friends during your time of need. ∎

HOMEBUILDERS

DEL WEBB SWEETGRASS

LOVE LIFE TO THE FULLEST ™

Del Webb®

3031 Persimmon Grove
Richmond, Texas 77469
(281) 866 6072
www.delwebb.com/houston

There's a unique spirit you'll experience in a Del Webb community. Whether it's getting in touch with your muse in a painting class, being part of a volunteer group or taking advantage of opportunities for lifelong learning, you'll be amazed at how rich life can be here. Del Webb has been a leader in active-adult living for more than 50 years, and you'll get to experience that firsthand at Del Webb Sweetgrass in Richmond, Texas.

Del Webb Sweetgrass is set amid rolling topography with 80 acres of open space and 50 acres of water, including Rabb's Bayou. In the center of it all is the Lakehouse, on schedule to open in spring 2012. The Lakehouse will be the hub of activity, featuring 27,000 square feet of space just waiting for you to come and play. With a state-of-the-art fitness center, resort-style pool, grand ballroom, demonstration kitchen, high-tech learning classroom, event lawn, outdoor amphitheater and outdoor kitchen, the enjoyment opportunities are endless.

But it doesn't stop with the property. A full-time lifestyle coordinator is there to ensure that the calendar is bursting with fun. Typical activities include volunteering and charity work, travel and book clubs, dance and theatre and simply getting to know others in the community at happy hour. Del Webb offers a lifestyle that is second to none.

Living at Sweetgrass means life is built for you, and that means the homes, too. Del Webb Sweetgrass offers a variety of single-story floor plans designed with the active adult in mind. You'll find larger living spaces for entertaining, fewer bedrooms and special attention to flex spaces, such as outdoor areas and hobby rooms. With homes ranging from the $140s at around 1,100 square feet to $250,000 at around

HOMEBUILDERS

2,700 square feet, you are sure to find the perfect home for your needs.

There's really only one way to see what Del Webb is truly about, and that's to come see for yourself. Located just south of Sugar Land on Highway 59 at exit 762 north, Del Webb Sweetgrass will be on your right.

Come and love life to the fullest™. ■

OPPOSITE: The Del Webb Sweetgrass entrance monument glows at dusk.

ABOVE: (clockwise from top left) Ornamental grass on the property; common-area fire pit near Rabb's Bayou; Rabb's Bayou at sunrise; Dunwoody Way model; Morningside Lane model.

HOMEBUILDERS

CHESMAR HOMES

SETTING A HIGHER STANDARD

CHESMAR HOMES
Setting a Higher Standard

450 Gears Road, Suite 400
Houston, Texas 77067
(281) 598-1111
www.chesmar.com

Chesmar Homes is known for designing functionality and high-performance into homes it builds using cutting-edge building science techniques. Branded as **MPG** [**M**odern Design - **P**erformance Guaranteed - **G**reen Certified^SM], it means that each Chesmar home is guaranteed to use less energy, cost less to operate, and provide a comfortable environment.

Chesmar associates core discipline is doing what they say they will do. Don Klein, President and founder of Chesmar Homes says he is living out his dream everyday. "At Chesmar, we build homes because we love to build homes. It is our passion...our profession of choice. Our professional team is top-notch; each is dedicated to creating neighborhoods and homes of distinction while providing an excellent customer experience. Our family style culture centers around taking care of each other and making it our goal to have fun along our way to success!"

Since establishment in 2005, Chesmar has built and closed more than 2000 homes in many of Houston's premier communities. Among its many achievements is the development of seven different product series, having earned the Builder 100 designation, as well as receiving a Builder of the Year recognition by the Greater Houston Builders Association.

Community support is central to Chesmar Homes. The company is most notably known for its vigorous support of the GHBA Benefit Home Project, having partnered with developers and vendors to build three homes in three consecutive years, the proceeds of which benefit HomeAid Houston, Texas Children's Cancer Center, and Alzheimer's Association, Houston. Learn more about Chesmar Homes at **www.chesmar.com**. ∎

HOMEBUILDERS

TRENDMAKER

PROVIDING A SUPERIOR HOME BUYING EXPERIENCE

16340 Park Ten Place, Suite 250
Houston, Texas 77084
(281) 675-3200
TrendmakerHomes.com

Trendmaker Homes proudly celebrated its 40th Anniversary in 2011. There is only one way a company can survive and thrive for four decades, and that is by satisfying its customers. We are extremely proud of the success we've enjoyed these past 40 years and satisfied customers will remain the heart and soul of our company for the next 40 years and beyond.

Trendmaker has long been recognized as one of Houston's premier new home builders. Throughout the years, we've defined the concept of a luxury home for generations of Houstonians. Unlike some new homebuilders who build every kind of home for every kind of buyer, Trendmaker has focused on the needs and desires of the most discriminating homebuyers, and the results have been spectacular. After 40 years of being one of Houston's most trusted builders, Trendmaker has grown and adapted for our buyers and for the constantly changing housing market.

Avanti Custom Homes by Trendmaker is our latest building program which allows us to fill even more building niches for our customers. More than just a "Build On Your Lot" program, Avanti Custom Homes offers full design services, access to a large collection of customizable plans or the ability to work with our buyer's plans. Buyers now can have a Trendmaker anywhere, in any setting, within the greater Houston area whether coastal, urban, suburban, or estates.

In addition to Avanti Custom Homes, Texas Casual Cottages by Trendmaker are being built in the beautiful Texas Hill Country. We now offer two model home parks that showcase these homes with extensive landscaping, outdoor pergolas, seating areas, fire pits, carriage houses, and much more. The popular Round Top area is the location of our first model home park, which also won the Greater Houston Builder's Association Houston's Best Award for Model Home Park of the Year. Our second and newest model home park is located in Wimberley, Texas. Whether you're looking for a weekend retreat or a new home in the country, Texas Casual Cottages offers a wide variety of plans and options to accommodate our buyer's lifestyles.

For more information on Trendmaker's communities or any of our building programs, visit **TrendmakerHomes.com**

INSURANCE COMPANIES

INSGROUP, INC.

ACTING FASTER, THINKING SMARTER, WORKING HARDER

INSURANCE | RISK MANAGEMENT | EMPLOYEE BENEFITS

1455 West Loop South, 9th Floor
Houston, Texas 77027
(713) 541-7272
www.insgroup.net

Insgroup, Inc., founded in 1978, has grown into one of the largest privately held insurance agencies in Texas. In 2010, the *Insurance Journal* listed the firm as a Top 100 Independent Insurance Agency in the United States, and the *Houston Business Journal* ranked Insgroup as the fifth largest Houston-based property/casualty insurance brokerage firm. As a regional broker, Insgroup is licensed to write property/casualty insurance in all 50 states, maintaining offices in Texas and Florida, with a growing professional staff of around 75 employees. Insgroup's clients range from private local firms to national organizations. The company has relationships with all major property/casualty carriers and employee benefits providers, and their clout in the marketplace enables them to obtain proposals from multiple carriers to ensure that their programs are both broad in scope and competitively priced. As a "full-service" firm, Insgroup is divided into four areas:

- **Commercial Insurance**: Insgroup places all lines of commercial property/casualty coverage and provides risk-management consulting and surety-bonding services. Insgroup has expertise in professional liability, directors and officers liability, environmental insurance, mergers and acquisitions coverage and foreign insurance. Industries Insgroup focuses on include real estate/hospitality, construction, manufacturing, energy and marine, transportation, technology, financial/professional services, health care, agribusiness and not-for-profit.

- **Marine and Aviation Insurance**: Insgroup places coverage on all types of vessels, including megayachts, cruisers and high-performance boats moored worldwide. In addition to pleasure craft, Insgroup provides comprehensive insurance programs for marinas, shipyards, terminals, commercial hull, P&I and cargo.

- **Personal Insurance**: Insgroup focuses on creating custom-crafted insurance and risk solutions for high net-worth individuals and families with risk-management needs beyond "off-the-shelf" products. Many of their clients own multiple residences, foreign property, private aircraft, yachts and large valuable collections. Individuals and families with such exposures need an insurance broker with specialized expertise.

- **Employee Benefits**: Insgroup designs and places comprehensive benefits programs, including group medical, group life, disability, dental, vision and other supplemental benefits. Insgroup has expertise with the design, placement and servicing of fully insured and self-funded plans.

In addition to insurance-program design and placement, Insgroup provides value-added services to reduce total cost of risk, including claims management, safety- and loss-prevention consulting and alternative risk-transfer consulting.

Providing "first-class" service to clients is Insgroup's first priority. The team at Insgroup welcomes your inquiries and looks forward to working with you.

INSURANCE COMPANIES

NATIONWIDE INSURANCE THE MAY GROUP

SERVING OUR FELLOW TEXANS WITH ON YOUR SIDE® SERVICE

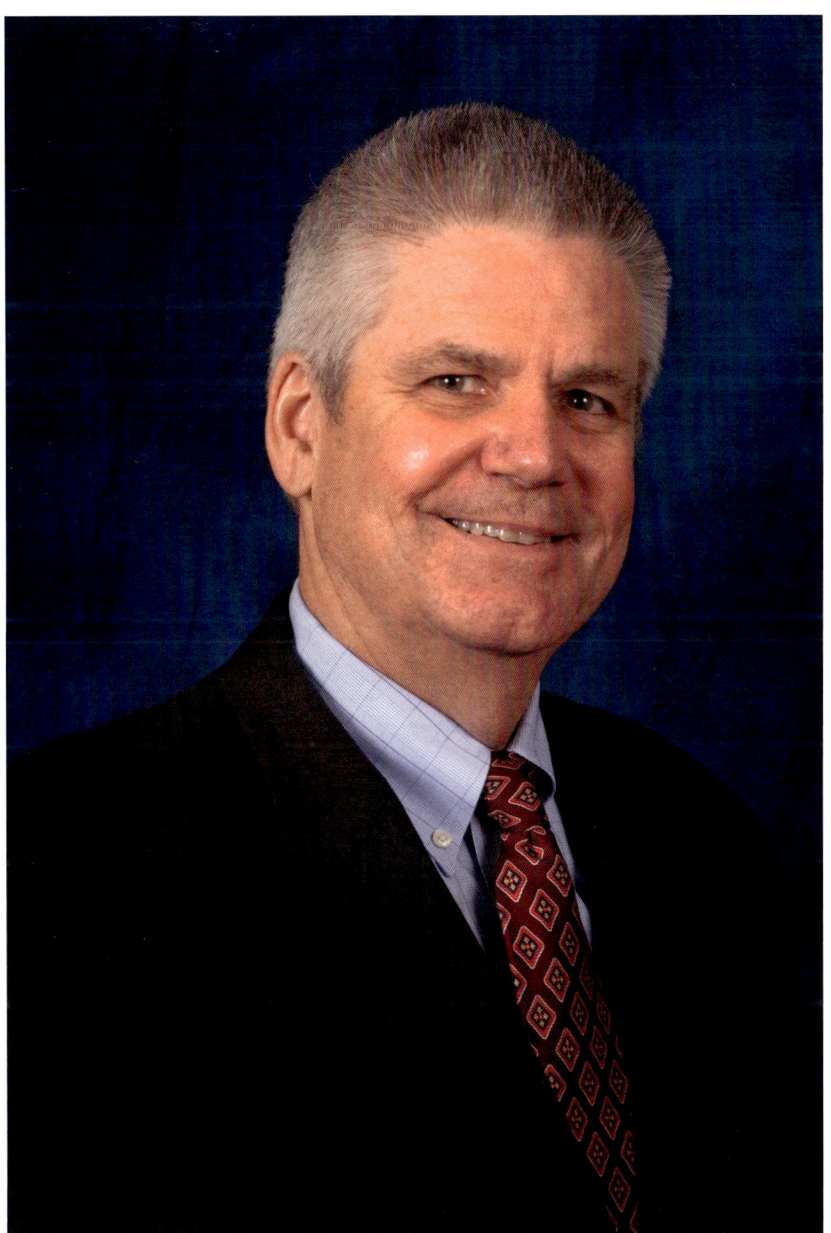

Tom May
Director of Operations
The May Group

730 North Post Oak Road, Suite 402
Houston, Texas 77024
(713) 807-8264
www.mayinsurancegroup.com

Founded in 1998 with one Houston location, The May Group, LLC, Insurance Services has grown to five branches in the Houston metropolitan area and two in San Antonio. We pride ourselves in providing our fellow Texans with On Your Side® service at all times.

The May Group is one of the fastest growing insurance agencies in the state. We currently have offices in Houston, Sugar Land, Katy and San Antonio. Each of our offices is staffed with experienced professionals who make customer service their first priority.

Direction of Operations Tom May and the rest of the team at The May Group stand ready to assist you with all of your insurance needs. Our goal is to give you a refreshing change in the consumer insurance experience. We want to be able to serve you however it works for you. Our Web site has extensive information if you want to search on your own, but some questions require personal answers so you can contact us in person, by telephone or fax or by e-mail.

We offer a wide array of insurance, including personal and business as well as farm and ranch insurance. We know everyone has a unique situation, and we can tailor an insurance package to fit your needs.

In addition, The May Group offers free continuing-education courses for realtors to gain a basic understanding of insurance in the residential market. The classes can be scheduled at your convenience and choice of location.

Do you know someone who may need our assistance in protecting his or her family or business? Take a look at our Referral Rewards program through which you can be entered into a monthly gift-card drawing just for referring us to others.

Call or drop by any of our locations to experience The May Group difference. We can provide you with a "no obligation" On Your Side review of your current insurance package as well as discuss your unique needs and goals.

If you would like information about our offices, team members or insurance quotes, visit www.mayinsurancegroup.com or call (877) 807-8264.

We look forward to speaking with you soon! ∎

MASTER-PLANNED COMMUNITIES

CALDWELL COMPANIES

DOING IT RIGHT, RIGHT NOW

7904 North Sam Houston
Parkway West, 4th Floor
Houston, Texas 77064

(713) 690-0000

www.caldwellcos.com

Caldwell Companies is thankful for the opportunity to serve the Houston community, in particular the northwest region of Houston, for the past 20 years. Our services range from brokerage to investment to development and in each business our focus remains the same – building community. It is our passion and calling to help our clients achieve their goals whether they are looking to sell a warehouse, lease new office space, build a medical facility, diversify an investment portfolio or sell a family land tract. Whatever the assignment may be, our firm leverages market knowledge, passion and experience to provide service that exceeds your expectations. At Caldwell, it's about our relationships and adding value, which is why our clients turn to us year after year.

Our commercial development team can help your company realize its goals of new construction or redevelopment. We bring cost-effective and time-sensitive methodologies to each stage of a project. We work hard to reduce construction and ownership costs so corporate occupancy costs are reduced and client profitability is increased.

In our residential developments we focus on enhancing the lives of our residents. Part art and part science, our efforts include building resort-style amenities and recruiting the best home builders, designers, planners and contractors to create a quality of life not available in other communities.

Our investment business focuses on providing stable, high quality returns to private equity investors. With a 20-year history of consistent investment returns, our company has gained the trust of many investors.

Throughout the history of our company, we have remained a part of our communities, reinvesting in smart, responsible growth. And it is the strategic combination of multiple service lines that allows Caldwell Companies to serve our clients in a way that offers value beyond that found at other firms. ■

MASTER-PLANNED COMMUNITIES

TOWNE LAKE

A COMMUNITY CONNECTED BY WATER

A Community Connected by Water

Welcome Center
18915 San Saba Creek Circle
Cypress, Texas 77433

For more information,
call: (281) 256-2772

www.townelaketexas.com

Towne Lake is quickly becoming the centerpiece of one of Houston's most sought-after areas. Bordered by 290, West Road and Barker Cypress Road, Towne Lake is in the heart of the Cypress-Fairbanks area, surrounded with restaurants, shopping and wonderful recreational opportunities.

When complete, Towne Lake will be the site of Houston's fourth largest lake. Towne Lake reflects its Texas-sized appeal with numerous amenities and spectacular lake views. Our 300+ acre lake, designed specifically for recreational use, is the heart of this beautiful community and lake access is provided for all residents. You will have every opportunity within Towne Lake to relax, play, exercise and invest time with your family, friends and neighbors. Take your boat out on the water for a day of waterskiing or tubing. Or perhaps, take the family by boat for dinner at one of our restaurants followed by a concert at our lakeside amphitheater. You might want a more mellow tour of the lake from your kayak or canoe. There are also numerous neighborhood parks, many of which are lakeside and include park-side docks. After a day on the lake, cool off in the pool while the kids play on the splash pad nearby. Feel free to play a set or two of tennis or exercise in the state-of-the-art fitness center.

But it's more than amenities – it's design as well. The exceptional homebuilders in Towne Lake embrace Texas charm with new home designs that honor the traditions of our state without sacrificing any of the modern features and luxuries that you desire.

Active adults looking to enjoy a resort lifestyle will discover that The Heritage at Towne Lake, our neighborhood area exclusively for those 55 and better, is a bustling community with convenient services, amenities and planned social activities that knit neighbors together. No matter your age, Towne Lake has something for everyone. And then some! ∎

MASTER-PLANNED COMMUNITIES

FIRETHORNE

FIRETHORNE COMBINES VIBRANCY OF WEST HOUSTON WITH SMALL-TOWN CHARM OF KATY/FULSHEAR

For more information
call (281) 693-1011
or visit
www.firethorne.info

Firethorne is a 1,400-acre residential community designed to combine the vibrancy of West Houston with the small-town charm of Katy/Fulshear. Ranked in Houston Business Journal's Top 5 most active communities in the Houston area, Firethorne is strategically located on FM 1463, near the crossroads of the I-10 West corridor, the Westpark Tollway and the Grand Parkway.

Named for a resilient evergreen indigenous to the Texas prairie, Firethorne blends with the best nature has to offer: 150 acres devoted to parks and recreational amenities highlighted by a scenic 12-acre lake with surrounding greenbelt, hike and bike trails, parks and playgrounds, discovery-rich wildlife observation area, a natural bird habitat and more. Its 12-acre Lake Firethorne and hike/bike trails make it the ideal venue to host the Rotary Club of Katy's 19th Annual Katy Triathlon at Firethorne.

Family amenities include a resort-style multi-level family swim center, sports fields (featuring the Houston area's only regulation lacrosse playing field), a neighborhood Community Center with a meeting room, a fully equipped fitness facility and a new competitive Swim Center with regulation six-lane, 25-yard-long lap pool.

The Firethorne builder team consists of Ashton Woods Homes, M/I Homes, Perry Homes, Highland Homes, Plantation Homes and Coventry Homes. New homes range in price from the high $100s to the mid-$800s. The builder team members have been selected based upon the highest standards for design, quality, customer satisfaction and reputation.

With opportunities for nature discovery all around, plus being located in the acclaimed Katy Independent School District (Katy ISD) and Lamar Consolidated Independent School District, Firethorne is rooted in the spirit of learning. Katy I.S.D. has begun construction on Firethorne's first elementary school, with completion targeted for the start of the 2012-13 school year.

Kindle your spirit at Firethorne, situated 10 and 15 miles west, respectively, of the Texas Medical Center-West Campus and Houston's Energy Corridor. To tour, take I-10 West and exit Pin Oak to FM 1463, visit **www.firethorne.info**, or call 281-693-1011.

MASTER-PLANNED COMMUNITIES

CROSS CREEK RANCH
THE "PERFECT BLEND" OF EVERYTHING YOU WANT IN A COMMUNITY

Cross Creek Ranch
Welcome Center
6450 Cross Creek Bend Lane
Fulshear, Texas 77441

MON - SAT: 10 am - 6 pm
SUN: 12 noon - 5 pm

For more information,
call: (281) 344-9882
CrossCreekTexas.com

Over 600 happy homeowners now call Cross Creek Ranch home. A premier 3,200 acre master-planned community located on Houston's popular westside, just south of Katy in Fulshear, Texas, Cross Creek Ranch offers the "perfect blend" of everything you want in the place you'll call home.

A Trendmaker Development community, Cross Creek Ranch features authentic small town charm along with a wide variety of resort-style amenities including a spectacular Water Park with a large swimming pool, a 200ft. water slide, a wading pool for the little ones, and a colorful Spray & Splash Pad; a deluxe, spacious Fitness Center with great views of the lakes and pool area; 100's of acres of beautiful lakes and green space; miles of hike-and-bike trails that wind along the lakes and through the neighborhoods; numerous neighborhood play parks for kids; an outdoor sports park with basketball and tennis courts; and much more. Cross Creek Ranch also features an innovative land plan design which benefits the environment and the residents including the planting of almost 25,000 trees to-date with more to come in the future.

This land plan also includes the extensive restoration of Flewellen Creek. When completed, Flewellen Creek Park will provide a beautiful, natural centerpiece that winds through and connects many of the community's neighborhoods.

New homes are offered from a group of the finest local and national home-builders with prices ranging from the $180's to over $1 Million.

Cross Creek Ranch won a number of the Greater Houston Builder's Association's "Houston's Best" awards at their recent 2011 Awards Gala including Master Planned Community of the Year, Best Recreation Center, Best Welcome Center, Best Landscaping Design, Best Interactive Sales Experience, and Best Website.

Visit our award-winning Welcome Center and Café and see us online at **CrossCreekTexas.com**.

MASTER-PLANNED COMMUNITIES

SILVER RANCH

TRANQUIL SETTINGS AND CUSTOM LIVING

SILVER RANCH

For more information visit
www.silverranch.com

Located in the heart of Katy, Texas, just 30 miles west of downtown Houston, this master-planned community provides a suburban sanctuary with easy access to the energized urban environment that Houston has to offer. The Silver Ranch community puts every need right at your fingertips with its proximity to the popular Katy Mills Mall, renowned medical centers, grocery stores and movie theaters. In addition, the community is in the highly sought-after Katy Independent School District, a leader in education excellence.

With a commitment to customer satisfaction, the Silver Ranch community partnered up with multiple homebuilders, including Brighton Homes, David Weekly Homes and Meritage Homes, to bring prospective residents the very best in quality and unique design. Each of the partnering homebuilders offers different, customizable floor plans and sizes, allowing homebuyers to personalize the luxurious home they want at an affordable price, ranging from the $140s to $300s.

The growing community of Silver Ranch was built with the idea of family comfort in mind. In addition to the homes themselves, the community offers stunning outdoor-living amenities for everyone to enjoy. You can stroll through the safe neighborhood on beautifully landscaped walking trails or have a large group over for a cookout at the covered Outdoor BBQ Pavilion. The community also features tennis courts and an interactive children's playground as well as a refreshing six-lane adult swimming pool and splash pad for the kids to cool off during those hot Texas summers.

No matter how you like to spend your time, Silver Ranch will provide a tranquil oasis that lets you leave the congested concrete jungle behind.

NEIGHBORHOODS AND CITIES

CITY OF NASSAU BAY

INCOMPARABLE WATERFRONT ON THE LEADING EDGE OF TECHNOLOGY

18100 Upper Bay Road
Nassau Bay, Texas 77058
(281) 333-4211
www.nassaubay.com

Hilton
Houston NASA Clearlake

3000 NASA Parkway
Houston, Texas 77058
(281) 333-9300
www.houstonnasaclearlake.hilton.com

Nassau Bay has always been at the center of the American Space Program. Adjacent to beautiful Clear Lake, Nassau Bay originally was developed to accommodate Johnson Space Center (JSC) and provide housing as well as other amenities to the astronauts, industry professionals and their families.

The City of Nassau Bay has blossomed into a major tourist destination with an estimated 2,500 people participating in a plethora of activities taking place at any given time. Some of the most popular events include the Annual Ballunar Festival, at which spectators can watch more than 100 hot air balloons take flight over NASA's Rocket Park, and the Wings Over Houston Airshow, where attendees can take in the experience of spectacular aerial performances. Other exciting attractions include Space Center Houston, where you can take tours of JSC, and the Clear Lake Recreation Area, the third largest boating center in the United States.

The City of Nassau Bay recently teamed up with Griffin Partners to create new development and began renovating the city in an effort to keep up with ever-growing tourism demands. The newly named Nassau Bay Town Square is a 31-acre mixed-use development located across from JSC that will feature three Silver LEED office buildings with approximately 500,000 square feet of space, a 313-unit multi-family project, a 124-suite Marriott Hotel, retail space, conference center and City Hall. The redesigned streets and promenade will have sidewalks and benches as well as charming landscaping to encourage pedestrian traffic.

Also recently renovated, the Hilton Houston NASA Clear Lake is a suburban resort where each suite has a view of magnificent Clear Lake. The hotel creates a relaxing environment for business and leisure travelers alike.

Come visit the newly renovated city of Nassau Bay. You might be surprised at what you'll find. ■

| Advertorial |

OIL & GAS – EQUIPMENT AND SERVICES

CAMERON
RAISING PERFORMANCE. TOGETHER™

1333 West Loop South, Suite 1700
Houston, Texas 77027
(713) 513-3300
www.c-a-m.com

Cameron is a leading provider of flow equipment products, systems and services to worldwide oil, gas and process industries. We apply our expertise to address challenges and deliver results, all with a focus on providing total solutions and continuously raising customer performance. We're proud to call Houston home – the fourth-largest city in the U.S. and the world's energy capital. Houston has served us well as we've grown into the global company we are today.

PERFORMANCE THROUGH MARKET LEADERSHIP

Cameron is a dynamic Fortune 500 provider with annual revenues exceeding $6 billion. Our legacy of leadership spans almost two centuries, representing a history of mutual success with our customers.

Our organization is comprised of 10 operating divisions, each holding a leading position in most every market segment served, with a combined roster of more than 60 trusted product brands. Our 22,000+ employees work in 300+ locations across 100+ countries worldwide, with more employees working outside the U.S. than inside. Our network of sales, engineering, manufacturing and aftermarket services covers North and South America; Europe, Africa, Caspian and Russia; and Asia Pacific and the Middle East.

Cameron's heritage is ongoing, grounded in quality, reliability and value. Cameron's capabilities lie in the understanding of customer needs, the application of technology, the anticipation of future challenges and the power to solve problems resourcefully. Cameron's brand is all about raising performance.

OIL & GAS – EQUIPMENT AND SERVICES

PERFORMANCE THROUGH WORLD-CLASS SERVICE

At Cameron, we know performance equals time and money. Delivering customer-specific solutions, Cameron deploys our expertise from upstream to downstream in nine distinct market segments: Onshore Drilling; Offshore Drilling; Onshore Production; Offshore Production; Subsea Production; Topsides Processing; Transmission and Storage; Refining, Petrochemical and LNG; and Industrial.

Our products and systems control, direct, adjust, process, measure and compress pressure and flows – all backed by CAMSERV™, Cameron's worldwide aftermarket network. From installation to decommissioning, CAMSERV provides comprehensive support for parts, service, repair, remanufacture and asset management.

PERFORMANCE THROUGH SOLID EXECUTION

Cameron maintains its leadership by doing things right. At Cameron, we are committed to what we believe to be right competencies.

The caliber, diversity and resourcefulness of Cameron's employees inspire pride as well as respect – proactive, experienced, savvy, creative team members. We attribute the quality of our work directly to the quality of our people.

Cameron's financial strength makes us one of the most respected companies in our industry. Shareholders invest in us because we are committed to managing our business and being effective stewards of assets. We are proud of our ability to perform in robust markets and to prove ourselves in less-than-ideal times.

With the goal of making constant improvement in quality and productivity, Enterprise Excellence builds on Cameron's established Lean Six Sigma methodology, tools and support to improve manufacturing and business processes company-wide.

We are committed to the sustainable creation of positive change, exceptional performance and lasting value. Cameron's Corporate Responsibility has four initiatives: To Sustain Economic Growth, To Build Our Communities, To Protect Health and Safety, To Preserve Our Environment. ■

OIL & GAS – EQUIPMENT AND SERVICES

FMC Technologies

LEADING GLOBAL PROVIDER OF TECHNOLOGY SOLUTIONS FOR THE ENERGY INDUSTRY

FMC Technologies

1803 Gears Road
Houston, Texas 77067
(281) 591-4000

www.fmctechnologies.com

FMC Technologies is a leading global provider of technology solutions for the energy industry. We have approximately 12,500 employees at 27 production facilities in 16 countries, where we design, manufacture and service technologically sophisticated equipment such as subsea production and subsea processing systems; high-pressure fluid control equipment; surface wellhead systems; measurement solutions; and marine loading systems for the oil and gas industry.

Our subsea technologies, and the value we provide customers can be categorized in three areas: field development, subsea processing and production enhancement. Whether it is high-pressure/high-temperature trees and wellheads, subsea controls or production optimization services, we add value to our customers throughout the life of the field, maximizing recovery rates and field investment dollars through the use of the industry's most innovative solutions.

A GLOBAL COMPANY WITH A LOCAL FACE

FMC's primary business is the development of subsea technologies that encompass a wide range of equipment and solutions necessary to operate offshore oil and gas fields. We are the industry leader by market share for subsea production equipment and we have a strong global presence in all of the world's major deepwater basins, including the Gulf of Mexico, North Sea, West Africa, Brazil and Asia Pacific regions.

In Africa, where most of the subsea projects are concentrated on the west coast of the continent, FMC has supported three of the region's largest deepwater projects to date. This includes Pazflor and CLOV, both operated by Total, as well as the Jubilee field operated by Tullow.

In the Asia Pacific region, subsea activity is mainly concentrated offshore Australia, Indonesia and Malaysia. FMC supports the most active operators in this region, including customers Chevron, Conoco Phillips, Murphy, Shell, Woodside and others. FMC also has alliance agreements with Woodside in Australia and a global supply agreement with Shell that have resulted in our significant presence in the area's highest profile projects. This includes Shell's Prelude development, a floating liquefied natural gas (FLNG) project using revolutionary technologies to access offshore gas fields that would otherwise be too costly or difficult to develop.

In the North Sea, exploration and development activities began in the southern part of the Norwegian Continental Shelf in the 1960s and continue to this day. Subsea developments started out as tie backs to existing platforms, which is still the case for smaller developments in the region. The North Sea has also been the origin of many of our current technology successes. For example, today, FMC has seven subsea separation projects across the world, where oil, gas, sand and water are separated at the seabed to reduce costs and allow operators to maximize production and

OIL & GAS – EQUIPMENT AND SERVICES

investment. All of these projects can trace their roots to Statoil's Tordis field in the North Sea, the world's first commercial application of a full-scale subsea separation system. Similar innovations continue today with technologies such as well intervention that can increase oil recovery, and systems designed to support Arctic projects that have resulted in FMC being selected to provide subsea systems for Gazprom's Kirinskoye field, Russia's first subsea project.

Petrobras, the national oil company of Brazil, is also the main offshore operator in that country, where approximately 600 subsea wells are producing oil and gas. A majority of those wells include subsea production systems supplied by FMC Technologies, including Petrobras' Marlim and Congro/Corvina fields. FMC Technologies' involvement in projects offshore Brazil also include systems installed at Chevron's Frade field and Shell's Parque das Conchas. The region is evolving into one of the world's largest offshore areas, and will be supported by our recently constructed South America Technology Center in Rio de Janeiro.

Closer to home, the Gulf of Mexico has continually presented some of the world's most promising and unique field discoveries. FMC has been at the forefront of providing innovative solutions for customers in the Gulf for decades, and today our reliable systems are used in high-pressure / high-temperature reservoirs where the hydrocarbons can exceed 350 degrees Fahrenheit and pressure flow can reach 15,000 psi. Examples of recent projects that FMC has supported include the three largest fields in the Gulf – BP's Thunder Horse, ExxonMobil's Hadrian and Shell's Perdido developments. The Perdido field also is the location of the world's current deepwater completion record, where an FMC subsea system was placed into production 9,356 feet – or nearly two miles – below the surface.

PEOPLE, TECHNOLOGY AND PERFORMANCE

FMC Technologies is backed by more than a century of accomplishments in a wide range of complex and exacting business specialties. While there is great strength in the diversity of our business and product portfolio, there is a common denominator that ties each of our businesses together – knowledge-based solutions engineering and a commitment to attracting and retaining the most talented workplace in the industry. ∎

LEFT: FMC's subsea processing systems, like the pictured equipment installed at Statoil's Tordis field in the North Sea, perform separation of oil, gas and water on the seabed, helping customers increase production and recovery rates.

ABOVE: FMC's multi-well pad drilling minimizes the environmental footprint of operations by using one dedicated site to drill and complete wells and recover the hydrocarbons.

BELOW: FMC's global reach extends to all of the world's most active deepwater basins, including Chevron's Agbami project, Nigeria's largest deepwater development.

OIL & GAS – EQUIPMENT AND SERVICES

KEY ENERGY SERVICES, INC.

WELL SERVICES • FLUID MANAGEMENT AND LOGISTICS
INTERVENTION SERVICES • FISHING AND RENTAL SERVICES

Key Energy Services
1301 McKinney, Suite 1800
Houston, Texas 77010
(713) 651-4300

www.keyenergy.com

Key Energy Services is the largest onshore, rig-based well servicing contractor based on the number of rigs owned, providing a complete range of oil and gas well intervention services. These include an advanced array of industry innovations that help improve the safety, quality and efficiency of the work performed. Key offers rig services, fluids management services, fishing and rental services and coiled tubing services.

Based in Houston, Texas, Key has operations in all major onshore oil and gas producing regions of the continental United States, as well as internationally in Mexico, Colombia, the Middle East, Russia and Argentina. Nearly 10,000 employees work from hundreds of domestic and international locations.

The company's services are primarily focused on helping its customers increase oil and natural gas production. This begins with having a quality workforce that is among the best trained in the industry and the right equipment to get the job done. Key operates a large fleet of over 860 well service rigs with horse-power ratings ranging from 150 up to 1,000. That fleet is built and maintained with one of the most extensive and aggressive remanufacturing programs in the industry. The result is more capable equipment built to improve safety, reduce downtime, and lower operating costs.

Key's well servicing operations continue assisting customers interested in maximizing value from plays with declining production. Additionally, Key's new-age well intervention operations include live well operations, heavy workovers, horizontal well completions, horizontal re-entries from vertical wellbores, specialized drilling services, long-lateral, extended-reach coiled tubing capabilities, large-scale fluid logistics management services and well testing. Key employs these techniques with industry-leading expertise and with more advanced technology than has ever been used before on well service equipment.

One example is the KeyView® System, a computer technology that is installed directly onto Key's rigs for monitoring well operations and capturing vital activity data. Customers and Key technicians can use this data to improve efficiency, quality and safety. It also provides for transparency and job data in a way that the industry has never had before. But not just Key customers are benefiting from the KeyView® System; Key is revolutionizing the well servicing industry by becoming a more technology-driven company. Continual research and development result in rigs being refined and upgraded with advancements that further improve best practices. ∎

OIL & GAS – EQUIPMENT AND SERVICES

SCHLUMBERGER OILFIELD SERVICES

INVESTING IN TECHNOLOGY FOR THE FUTURE

Schlumberger

300 Schlumberger Drive
Sugar Land, Texas 77478

www.slb.com

Schlumberger is the world's leading oilfield services company, supplying technology, integrated project management and information solutions to customers in the oil and gas industry worldwide. Schlumberger boasts a diverse, global workforce of 110,000 employees with 140 nationalities dedicated to delivering innovative solutions that improve production, increase reserves and reduce risk for international oil and gas customers.

Schlumberger has been a vital part of Houston since 1934 when company founder Conrad Schlumberger first came to Texas to establish North American operations for the company, founded in Paris in 1927. Greater Houston is now home to approximately 9,500 Schlumberger employees. Houston-based operations include U.S. corporate offices, the North American management team, operation and support services and key technology centers.

KEY TECHNOLOGY CENTERS

The 200-acre Sugar Land campus houses several hundred employees, and Schlumberger also has offices and facilities throughout the Houston area, including five of the more than 25 global technology centers, which develop and manufacture Schlumberger proprietary products and solutions. A recent merger with Smith International has expanded Schlumberger's key services and products to include drill bits, drilling tools, remediation services and drilling fluids. The combination of both companies' technologies serves has a catalyst for delivering more efficient and effective drilling services while reducing risk and optimizing drilling performance and well productivity for customers.

SUPPORTING HOUSTON AND THE INDUSTRY

Schlumberger maintains connections to the oil and gas industry with involvement in technical and business initiatives as well as charitable efforts. A corporate member of business societies—American Petroleum Institute and the Independent Petroleum Association of America (IPAA)—and professional societies—Society of Petroleum Engineers and American Association of Petroleum Geologists—Schlumberger has representatives actively helping drive and address oil and gas industry issues. Schlumberger also supports industry charities, such as Offshore Energy Center and Spindletop International as well as the Shell Houston Open and Junior Achievement.

COMMUNITY AFFAIRS

Schlumberger community affairs initiatives always have been part of our culture. Houston efforts are employee-driven and -identified areas of concern: education, wellness and environmental stewardship.

- Engineering Week, CSTEM Robotics Competition and IPAA's Petroleum Academy are initiatives focusing on science, technology, engineering and mathematics for students in Grades K–12 supported in partnership with local energy companies and universities.

- For wellness, employees support the Derricks & Diamonds charity softball tournament for Texas Children's Hospital Charity Care Program and Cancer Center, MS 150, American Heart Association's Heart Walk, Susan G. Komen Race for the Cure, and Juvenile Diabetes Research Foundation's Walk to Cure Diabetes.

- Environmental efforts include partnerships with the Nature Conservancy and the Houston Arboretum and Nature Center to support efforts and events in Houston. ■

OIL & GAS – EXPLORATION

CITGO PETROLEUM CORPORATION

HEADQUARTERED IN HOUSTON

1293 Eldridge Parkway
Houston, Texas 77077
(832) 486-4000
www.citgo.com

Headquartered in Houston, Texas, CITGO Petroleum Corporation is a refiner, marketer and transporter of gasoline, diesel fuel, jet fuel, lubricants, petrochemicals and other petroleum-based industrial products. CITGO has 3,700 employees and is owned by PDV America, Inc., a Delaware corporation and an indirect, wholly owned subsidiary of Petróleos de Venezuela, S.A. (PDVSA), the national oil company of the Bolivarian Republic of Venezuela.

CITGO owns and operates three highly complex crude oil refineries located in Lake Charles, La. (425,000 barrels-per-day [bpd]); Lemont, Ill. (167,000-bpd) and Corpus Christi, Texas (157,000-bpd). Our refineries process approximately 285,000-bpd of Venezuelan crudes, including supplies from Orinoco Oil Belt upgraders.

Our combined aggregate crude oil refining capacity of 749,000-bpd positions us as one of the largest refiners in the United States. We also own and/or operate 48 petroleum product terminals, one of the largest networks in the country. We market motor fuels to independent marketers who consistently rate CITGO as one of the best branded supplier companies in the industry. We also market jet fuel directly to airlines and produce agricultural, automotive, industrial and private label lubricants to independent distributors, mass marketers and industrial customers. In addition, we sell petrochemicals and industrial products directly to various manufacturers and industrial companies throughout the United States.

CITGO branded marketers sell motor fuels through approximately 6,100 branded retail outlets. In 2010, CITGO sold a total of 15.3 billion gallons of refined products.

OIL & GAS – EXPLORATION

HEATING OIL FOR THE POOR:
When the price of heating oil skyrocketed after Hurricanes Katrina and Rita, CITGO was the only company that responded to a request from U.S. senators to provide energy assistance to the most vulnerable. The CITGO-Venezuela heating oil program, which started as a one time donation, was created in 2005 to provide heating oil to needy individuals and the organizations that serve them. The 2010-2011 winter was the program's 6th consecutive season.

LIGHT BULBS TO HELP SAVE ENERGY:
The 2011 CITGO-Venezuela Energy Efficient Lighting Program (EELP) is providing 500,000 energy efficient compact fluorescent light bulbs (CFLs) to help approximately 50,000 low-income households in 17 U.S. cities, including Houston, save energy and contribute to the protection of the environment.

HUMANITARIAN RELIEF:
The people of CITGO have generously supported in recent times earthquake survivors in Haiti, those displaced by tornadoes in the U.S. southeast and flood victims in Venezuela. ∎

OPPOSITE LEFT: CITGO headquarters in the Energy Corridor, West Houston.

TOP RIGHT: CITGO refinery in Corpus Christi, Texas.

BOTTOM RIGHT: CITGO has 3,700 direct employees and through a network of more than 6,000 independently owned and operated retail locations, the company is part of a community of nearly 50,000 people.

OIL & GAS – EXPLORATION

CHEVRON
THE POWER OF HUMAN ENERGY

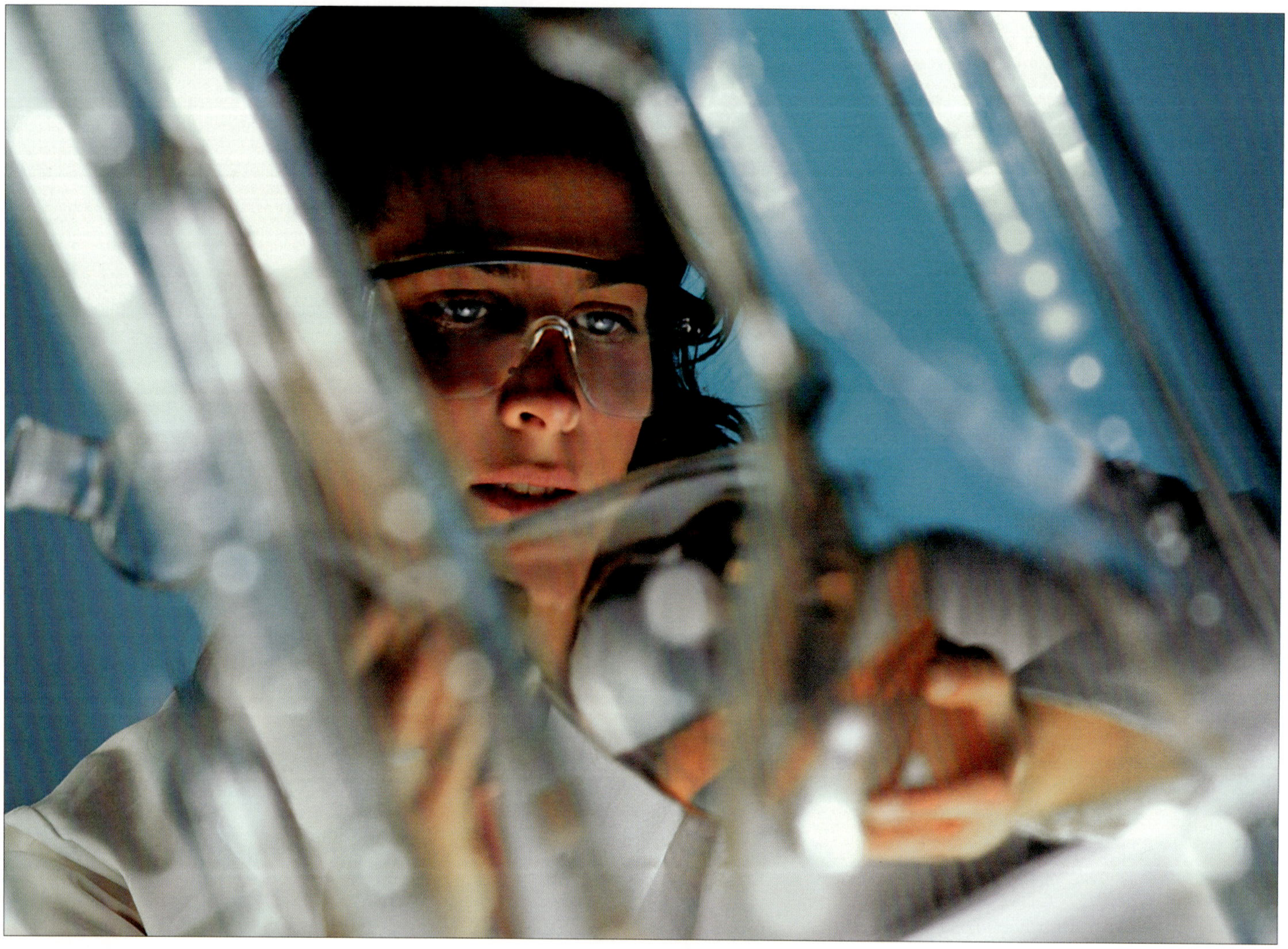

Human Energy™

Chevron Corporation
1400 Smith Street
Houston, Texas 77002
www.chevron.com

Chevron has been a company rooted in the business of exploring, developing and supplying energy for more than 130 years and is the second largest integrated energy company in the United States. We are engaged in virtually every aspect of the crude oil and natural gas industry, including exploration and production, manufacturing, marketing and transportation, chemicals manufacturing and sales, geothermal energy, and power generation.

The world needs all the energy we can develop, in every potential form. While finding new, safer and cleaner ways to maximize the use of traditional resources, we also depend on technology to produce emerging sources of energy.

Nearly 9,000 Houston-area Chevron professionals support all sectors of our business in order to provide the energy necessary to drive human progress. From scientists to engineers, project managers to analysts, and all of our professionals, Chevron brings a wealth of knowledge to the table in Houston that supports our global operations. We provide high-quality energy products to our customers, value to our investors, and through our direct involvement, benefit to the greater Houston community.

Investing in communities where we operate is one of our core values. Each year, Chevron operations in Houston commit millions of dollars and thousands of volunteer hours to non-profit organizations that address our region's most critical needs. We build homes for Habitat for Humanity, plant trees for Trees of Houston, teach in classrooms with Junior Achievement and provide meals to the hungry through the Houston Food Bank among many other community engagements.

Through our operations and community support efforts, we strive to create unparalleled partnerships as we do our part to make our community a better place. ■

PHYSICIANS

ORTHOPAEDIC ASSOCIATES, L.L.P.

TAKING CARE OF YOUR HEALTH

ORTHOPAEDIC ASSOCIATES, L.L.P.
ORTHOPAEDIC SURGERY & SPORTS MEDICINE

BELLAIRE - FOUNDATION
MEDICAL
(713) 650-6900

DOWNTOWN HOUSTON
(713) 650-6900

KINGWOOD - DIAGNOSTIC
AFFILIATES
(281) 358-4145

WEST HOUSTON - KATY
(281) 829-2000

www.OADOC.com

The physicians of Orthopaedic Associates, L.L.P. (OA), the oldest ongoing orthopaedic group in Houston, believe in the philosophy established by their founding fathers: a conservative approach to surgery, combined with personal attention, provides the best treatment of orthopaedic injuries. Founded in 1950, OA was formed to provide excellent orthopaedic treatment and surgery. State-of-the-art facilities located in downtown Houston, Bellaire, Kingwood, and in Katy, offer patients comprehensive treatment and surgery services close to home.

OA provides services for your entire family:

- Arthritis Surgery -
  Total Hip & Knee Replacement
  Total Shoulder & Elbow Replacement
- Arthroscopic Surgery
- Sports Injuries - Fractures/Broken Bones
- Reconstruction of Musculoskeletal Deformities
- Spine Specialists - Spine Disorders:
  Cervical & Lumbar
- Work-Related Injuries
- Pediatric, Adolescent, and Adult Orthopaedics

The practice specializes in spine and sports orthopaedics, as well as general orthopaedics. Besides their respective educational accomplishments, each physician is board certified by the American Board of Orthopaedic Surgeons, representing the highest standard available in the orthopaedic industry. OA surgeons rely on their colleagues' support and active participation in the University of Texas Medical School Teaching Program where they all hold faculty appointments. All physicians are on staff of various hospitals. The group's strength evolves from a special partnership – a team of physicians genuinely focused on bringing patients the best in care of orthopaedic injuries and abnormalities.

OA is a valued partner for many of America's largest managed healthcare companies, HMOs and PPOs, working in harmony with your primary care physician and health care provider. We provide immediate response to emergency orthopaedic services and specialized treatment programs, each designed to minimize patient pain and suffering. ∎

PORTS

PORT OF GALVESTON
GATEWAY TO THE GULF

123 Rosenberg Avenue, 8th Floor
Galveston, Texas 77550
(281) 286-2484
www.portofgalveston.com

Winner of the 2004 National Council for Public-Private Partnerships – Distinguished Public-Private Partnership Infrastructure Award.

Travel down Galveston Bay to where it meets the Gulf of Mexico at Galveston Island and you will find the Port of Galveston—"Your Gateway to the Gulf", located just 9.3 miles from the open sea. Originally established on land belonging to Mexico, the Port of Galveston is the oldest port in the Gulf of Mexico west of New Orleans. What began as not much more than a trading post located on the deepest natural harbor on the Texas Coast in 1825 has burgeoned into a significant contributor to the economic strength and well-being of the Galveston-Houston region and the State of Texas.

Serving as the primary point of embarkation for cruises to the western Caribbean, the Port of Galveston is the Premier Cruise Port in the Gulf of Mexico and the "Cruise Capital of Texas." Nearly 900,000 cruise passengers annually access the Port and explore the Historic Downtown Galveston Strand District before or after their voyage. The cruise industry, operating its ships from the Port of Galveston, contributed over $1.05 billion in direct spending and 15,541 jobs to the Texas economy in 2009.

In 2011 the Port of Galveston ranked as the only cruise ship port in Texas and #1 in the Gulf of Mexico, the 6th busiest cruise port in the U.S. and one of the top-twenty cruise home ports in the world. The Port is currently the year round "Home Port" to the Carnival Cruise Line ships, Carnival Magic and Carnival Triumph, and the seasonal "Home Port" to Royal Caribbean International's Mariner of the Seas. September 2011 marked the 11th anniversary of Carnival Cruise Lines sailing from the Port of Galveston.

In 2011 the Port of Galveston sent its two previous long-serving Carnival ships to New Orleans and welcomed the arrival of two new Carnival Cruise Lines ships. Carnival Magic, the newest ship built for the line's fleet, and Carnival's Flagship, holds 3,690 passengers and offers 7-day cruises to the eastern and western Caribbean beginning in November 2011. Carnival Triumph, which holds 2,758 passengers, moved from New Orleans to Galveston to offer year-round four- and five-day Caribbean cruises starting October 6, 2011. Also in November 2011, the Royal Caribbean International ship Mariner of the Seas arrived in Galveston to conduct 7-day winter season cruises, replacing its older sister ship, Voyager of the Seas, which also moved to New Orleans. In the Fall of 2012, the cruise ships Crown Princess and Disney Magic will arrive and sail with itineraries from the Port of Galveston.

The Port of Galveston, with over 850 acres located on Galveston and adjacent Pelican Island, also facilitates a diverse mix of domestic and international cargo that delivers value to the region and the state. The Port is a self supporting enterprise with current annual operating revenues of approximately $23 million.

The Port of Galveston is only 45 minutes from Downtown Houston and 30 minutes from the Gulf of Mexico by water, making it ideally accessible for business and Galveston Island enjoyment. ■

REALTORS

THE GRETZER GROUP

RECRUITMENT SUPPORT, RELOCATION & REAL ESTATE FOR HEALTHCARE PROFESSIONALS

(L-R) Barbara D. Gretzer, Broker, Owner; Linda Boylan Miller, Realtor Associate, Administrator; Mary T. Davenport, Broker Associate

THE GRETZER GROUP

7734 Portal Drive
Houston, Texas 77021
(713) 777-5932
www.gretzergroup.com

The Gretzer Group has successfully recruited and relocated thousands of professionals in the healthcare industry, helping to shape Houston and the Texas Medical Center as a renowned and leading source of healthcare services and research. By attracting world-class professionals through an alliance of specialists who provide recruitment support, relocation and real estate services, The Gretzer Group guarantees their clients a commitment of excellence.

Recognizing the unique lifestyle needs of healthcare professionals, The Gretzer Group has become an essential partner with medical institutions and companies to assess, develop and implement recruitment and relocation policies. Tailored programs meet the specific objectives, needs, and goals of each client.

The designed framework systematically accomplishes a fruitful recruitment with comprehensive area orientation, cost effective real estate transactions, monetary savings for the candidates, and assured retention. Additional support is offered throughout the process to ensure a stress free transition and it is this level of dedication which often leads to clients continuing to utilize The Gretzer Group's real estate services and recommending them to their friends and family members. The Gretzer Group's un-matched attention to detail has garnered national attention.

Since **Barbara Gretzer** established The Gretzer Group over fifteen years ago, she and her organization have not only contributed to Houston's healthcare community but to patients who benefited from such exceptional medical care as well. As a board member of the Texas Medical Center Orchestra, Barbara has worked with this community orchestra to bring musical entertainment to the public as well as raise funds for local charities through its concerts. Barbara was also instrumental in developing the TMC Orchestra's Gran Fondo for April, 2012. ∎

| Advertorial |

REALTORS

RE/MAX 360

PROVIDING FULL CIRCLE REAL ESTATE SERVICES

RE/MAX® 360

3033 Chimney Rock, Suite 100
Houston, Texas 77056
(832) 333-0360
(832) 875-7301 Mobile
thaiklam@remax360.com
www.REMAX360.com

Deciding to sell or buy a home is a big step. To make sure it's a step in the right direction, you need to choose the person best qualified to handle your real estate needs: a RE/MAX 360 Sales Associate. RE/MAX 360 is a company built on the promise of exceptional customer service. Whether you are selling your home or searching for that special place to call your own, you deserve to work with someone who has your best interests in mind.

Since RE/MAX 360s office opened, Thai Klam and his agents focus on growth and business development. Thai currently predicts over one hundred twenty million in sales by the end of this year and is expecting to double that in 2012. Averaging three times the production and more advanced industry education than other agents, RE/MAX 360 Associates are truly "The Real Estate Leaders®" in quality customer service. Customer satisfaction is reflected in our high, industry-leading rate of repeat and referral business.

In order to benefit their clients, Thai syndicates all RE/MAX 360 listings through dozens of different sites for both residential and commercial buyers. His agents develop and leverage their listings by creating videos in order to better promote their products. Thai and his agents realize that something as valuable as your trust must be earned. Whatever your particular real estate need, they will work hard to make sure that you are completely satisfied. RE/MAX 360 Sales Associates have the knowledge, experience and dedication that it takes to get you results.

When you choose a RE/MAX 360 Sales Associate to sell your home or help you purchase a new home, you will experience a whole new level of service. Thai and his agents at RE/MAX 360 are set on "Providing Full Circle Real Estate Services!" They will make you feel like one of the family. Consummate professionals, RE/MAX 360 Associates lead the industry in advanced real estate education and production. That is why they are known as "The Real Estate Leaders®" and why no one in the world sells more real estate than RE/MAX. ■

DAVID YOUNG TEAM

DEDICATED PROFESSIONALS DELIVERING THE REWARDS OF HOME OWNERSHIP

UNITED, REALTORS®
The David Young Team

14201 Memorial Drive, Suite 202
Houston, Texas 77079
(713) 722-6900
www.davidyoungteam.com

Buyers and Sellers deserve excellent representation and the guidance of professional Realtors® to navigate the complex real estate process. That is exactly what they receive when they are represented by the David Young Team. We specialize in working with Buyers and Sellers of real estate in all areas of Houston - from downtown Houston to Katy, from The Woodlands down to Sugar Land. Team members are experienced and individually successful Realtors®, supported by a full staff which provides clerical, advertising and graphic support.

For five consecutive years prior to forming the team, David H Young had been recognized by the *Houston Business Journal* as the #1 or #2 agent in the Greater Houston Area in dollar volume sales. In 2005, he leveraged this success by creating The David Young Team. The Team consists of ten successful real estate agents and two experienced assistants with expertise in all types of residential properties.

With average annual sales exceeding $100 million, The David Young Team continuously receives prestigious local and national recognition by the *Houston Business Journal* and Coldwell Banker. Since 2005, national awards ratings for Realtors have been sponsored by the *Wall Street Journal* and *Real Trends Magazine*. Each year the David Young Team ranked in the top 100 in sales volume placing them in the top one half of one percent of the more than one million Realtors nationwide.

We are honored to represent the Kickerillo Companies, Houston's largest custom home builder, as well as other quality builders in the greater Houston area. We earn repeat business through our knowledge, experience, professionalism and results, and look forward to helping you with all of your residential real estate needs. ■

WEALTH MANAGEMENT COMPANIES

ZT WEALTH

ONE DYNAMIC RESOURCE FOR ALL YOUR FINANCIAL NEEDS

1535 West Loop South, Suite 415
Houston, Texas 77027
(855) ZTALTUS (855-982-5887)
www.ztwealth.com

Securities offered through EDI Financial, Inc., Member FINRA/SIPC/MSRB Advisory Services offered through EDI Investment Advisor Corporation 12221 Merit Drive, Suite 1020 Dallas, TX 75251 (214) 528-4090

ZT Wealth, Inc. (or LLC) is not affiliated with EDI Financial, Inc./EDI Investment Advisor Corporation. The Independent Advisors and Independent Registered Representatives of ZT Wealth, Inc. (or LLC) are affiliated with EDI Financial, Inc./EDI Investment Advisor Corporation.

More than a decade ago, Taseer Badar founded ZT Wealth and began forging strong partnerships with clients seeking a comprehensive resource for financial freedom based on traditional, well-planned investing. Through the years, ZT's proven track record of financial success for their clients has garnered local and global recognition.

For 2012, ZT Wealth is rising to a new level of excellence. In the past year, they have seen increased exposure in the marketplace with more companies recognizing their success and desirable model as a private company and wanting to partner or do business with them. In the past year alone, nearly 25 companies have approached them with interest in merger or acquisition possibilities.

ZT Wealth carefully considers each proposal or project with their own growth in mind and the idea to merge and expand without losing their integrity or compromising quality of service.

This outside interest has enabled ZT Wealth to broaden their horizons into new branches of the health care sector and make them one of the fastest growing companies in Houston. In turn, this has opened new doors to investors worldwide who want to put their trust and money in proven, capable hands.

Projected to open in early 2012, ZT Wealth is constructing a half-million dollar office in the Galleria area of Houston housing the new ZT Wealth Sapphire Group. It will service exclusive, hand-selected, private clients.

WEALTH MANAGEMENT COMPANIES

For more than a dozen years, the financial and business experts at ZT Wealth have partnered with their clients to create, sustain and distribute wealth through a range of traditional, alternative, and equity-focused investments. Founded as a one-man operation, ZT Wealth has grown into a thriving institution backed by an advisory board and full support team, providing the resources to satisfy both your investment goals and risk tolerance for your business and personal portfolios.

Clients are able to diversify their portfolios with ZT Wealth's access to profitable projects not normally available to individual investors. In 2011, they raised more capital than ever, enabling them to reach an all-time record. A 2012 forecast shows that this record will be broken once again. Examples of their successful private-equity offerings are Shadow Creek Business Center and Global Properties ZT Wealth.

ZT Wealth has international resources to purchase, lease and manage turn-key residential and commercial properties. Through their strategic alliances they are opening the world of opportunity to their client-investors with both health care and real estate investments in the United States and abroad.

ZT Wealth forges strong partnerships with both their client-partners and the banking community. Through the years they have created a powerful network of banking relationships that enable them to advocate for their clients to get the most competitive rates available.

Altus Healthcare Management Services (Altus HMS) is a network of progressive physicians collaborating to achieve professional and financial growth through the creation, promotion and management of leading-edge health care facilities. They are a company by physicians and for physicians with a management team consisting of exceptional medical and financial specialists.

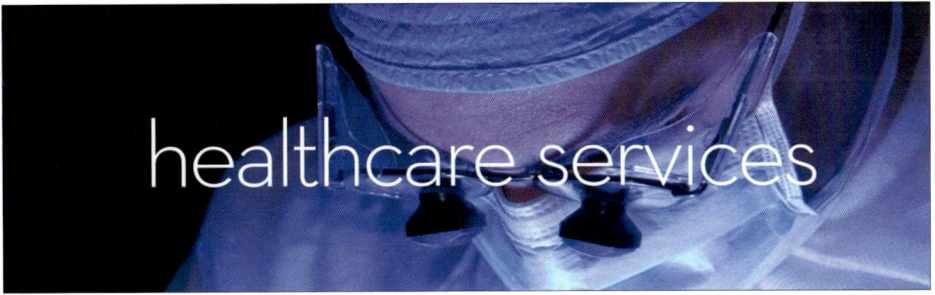

Despite a rise in health care spending, physicians suffer from a steady decline of professional fee distributions. Nonetheless, physicians continue to treat more patients and take on additional liability without a rise in compensation. Recognizing this inequity, the determined group of medical and financial specialists at ZT Wealth united to establish Altus HMS to ensure the health care dollar benefits healthcare professionals. ZT Wealth handles the daily business management so doctors can concentrate on what they do best: medical care. This unique medical business model is in successfully operating in multiple locations throughout Texas and has potential for worldwide application.

The Altus philosophy is simple: empowering physicians results in better healthcare and better business. By engaging physicians as key stakeholders in their health care management strategy, Altus HMS and ZT Wealth can deliver professional and financial benefits in return as well as make significant advancements through collaboration. The outcome is better care for patients. Altus HMS currently has a network of 700 physicians and is selectively growing.

To learn more about Altus HMS, visit www.altushms.com ■

| Advertorial |